IT'S
—
A
—
SLIPPERY
———
SLOPE
———

ALSO BY SPALDING GRAY

Sex and Death to the Age 14

Swimming to Cambodia

In Search of the Monkey Girl

Orchards

Monster in a Box

Impossible Vacation

Gray's Anatomy

SPALDING GRAY

IT'S
A
SLIPPERY
SLOPE

❄

THE NOONDAY PRESS

A division of Farrar, Straus and Giroux / New York

The Noonday Press
A division of Farrar, Straus and Giroux
19 Union Square West, New York 10003

Library of Congress Cataloging-in-Publication Data
Gray, Spalding, 1941–
    It's a slippery slope / Spalding Gray. — 1st ed.
        p.   cm.
    ISBN (invalid) 0-374-55524-5 (paper : alk. paper)
    1. Middle-aged men—United States—Drama.   2. Midlife crisis—
United States—Drama.   3. Fathers and sons—Drama.   4. Skiing—
Drama.   I. Title.
PS3557.R333I87   1997
812'.54—dc21   97-11634

Grateful acknowledgment to Paul Spencer, my creative consultant on the
original monologue; to Suzanne Gluck, for the title; to Martha Harrell,
who helped me teach my shadow to talk; and to Linda Greenburg and the
Vineyard Playhouse, Martha's Vineyard, where I first developed this text.

TO MY FAMILY —

Forrest, Marissa, Kathie, and Theo

IT'S
A
SLIPPERY
SLOPE

❄

✳

The first mountain I ever remember seeing was framed
in the pane of my geometry class window at Fryeburg
Academy in Maine in 1956. Well, I could hardly call it
a mountain; maybe it was twelve hundred feet high. But
it seemed like a mountain to one who came from Rhode
Island, the flatlands.

It was my first relief, and I needed relief. I was failing
all my subjects at Barrington High School, and my father
said, "Either you go away to Fryeburg Academy or you'll
end up in the Navy." So off I went to the Gulag, where
I was taking all the college preparatory courses including
geometry. And I was failing geometry, because I could
not stop staring out the window at a mountain. I could
feel the mountain pulling in my stomach. I was fasci-
nated by this thing, this mountain, because it looked like
an exotic dessert. I could see these white fingers through
the trees like melted marshmallow sauce over coffee ice
cream. And I couldn't figure out how the top of the

mountain could look like that until I discovered that those white fingers were ski runs and that the Fryeburg ski team practiced there. I also found out that if you went to Fryeburg Academy you could take free ski lessons. But you had to pass geometry in order to get into college and I thought I was failing geometry and couldn't go to college, so how could I ever afford to ski?

So instead of ski lessons I would go back to my room and fantasize about skiing. I would go back to my dorm room and daydream about skiing while I listened to Beethoven's symphonies, nine of them. One a day and three on Sundays. My room was so much warmer, because then, in 1956, in Fryeburg, Maine, we still had winter. There were 15-foot-high snowbanks along the road and 30-degree-below-zero temperatures, not counting the windchill factor. At night you could hear the elm trees SNAP outside your window, cracking from the cold like a .30/.30 rifle shot. And I was failing geometry. And I failed. I failed geometry, but somehow, I don't know how, Boston University accepted me. Maybe they needed more students that year or they didn't check my grades. So off to Boston I went, off to the big city!

This was very exciting for me. I forgot all about Maine and the mountains. Now I was living in Miles Standish Hall, the B.U. dorm in Kenmore Square. I was on the seventh floor, the highest I had ever been in my life. And it was a very traumatic experience, because my bed was right by the window. I would keep rearranging it, but the dorm room was so small that no matter where I moved the bed, it ended up by the window. It was disturbing because at the time I was taking Psychology 101 and I was reading about Freud for the first time and I read that he had discovered the unconscious. This was shocking to me. I had grown up thinking that I was all here. I didn't know that there was a big part of me that was an "un." I mean, there is no such thing as a little "un." I began to think that my unconscious harbored the self-destructive shadow in me which made me afraid to go to sleep at night because I thought my "un" would wake up, take over my body, and jump out the window with it, and halfway down, my conscious self would wake up and I'd be tearing at the brick walls trying to stop my fall. At last I became so upset by this that I transferred down the road to Emerson College, which had two-story dormitories not unlike the house I had grown up in in Barrington, Rhode Island.

Now this move to Emerson was unexpectedly important for me because it was there that I discovered my passion—at Emerson I finally found something that I was interested in—and that was theater. I wanted to become an actor. That is what I wanted to be. Then, I thought, I could live a passionate life onstage without consequences. I wouldn't have to make a choice of who I wanted to be. I could be a doctor, a lawyer, a father, a lover, a killer, a cop. I could be a Russian writer who shoots himself in the head one night and comes back the following night to shoot himself again. I wanted to be and "not be." Oh, for the glorious imitation of life! I thought that was it, I would act onstage, then come home, have a couple of beers, veg out, make it through—DIE—without ever having had to live—that was my ambition.

So after I got out of college I pursued acting for a while, but it started to wear thin very quickly, and what began to come up in me and push out this actor was the writer's voice—the need to create my own text—and I could not possibly figure out what that could be about, because I didn't know how to write or spell and I thought a writer had to be able to write. At the same time, I was constantly reshaping the playwright's words. I was not able to memorize them properly, I was paraphrasing. I constantly wanted to get my own text going. And what I did was start to move the acting into a monologue form in which I became a kind of inverted Method actor. I was using myself to play myself—I was playing with myself—a kind of creative narcissism.

I began to study myself as material, and out of that process I developed a series of autobiographic monologues. The first one I did was in 1979 in the Performing Garage in New York City and it was called *Sex and Death to the Age 14*—nothing too disturbing, basically masturbation and the death of goldfish. But these memories led to other memories and the monologues began to develop.

At the time I was developing these monologues I was living with Ramona. She was very helpful and supportive in my work and would often tour with me when I took monologues out on the road. At other times I would just go out on the road. I liked traveling with Ramona, who was highly structured and organized, so we would never get lost, we would never get lost with Ramona at the helm—but a part of me liked the adventure of getting lost and falling into the serendipitous synchronistic soup of life.

When I was out on the road alone I would often fall into other people's dramas, which they would create to ensnare me. Or I would create dramas for others and also have wild sexual encounters with strange women or strange sexual encounters with wild women. And I liked the variety of the security and then the insecurity, and bouncing back and forth between Ramona and not Ramona; it was fun. It was as if the monologue was a magic carpet I would go out to see the world with, and I would go wherever they asked me to, I was never picky—Austin, Aspen, wherever; you know, you go there and you find out what it's all about when you get there.

So we got this booking to bring my monologue *Monster in a Box* to Aspen, Colorado, and I took it.

What did I think of Aspen when I thought about it, I don't know—maybe cocaine. Those lines—that snow—Ramona and I were flying out of Denver on one of those little nineteen-seater planes, and I was looking out the window—it was sunset, I remember—and all of a sudden I looked down and "Oh! Oh my God, look at the size of those mountains. Ramona, are we in America? Look at those white beauties!" And that pull in my gut came again big-time, like in Fryeburg, Maine, but much stronger. Luckily there was a window there. This was unbelievable! Oh sure, I had flown over the Rocky Mountains to California thirty-five thousand feet up, but never down this low, where I could feel that big pull. Then there we were in Aspen, Colorado, me pacing back and forth in the Jerome Hotel like a moonstruck lad and looking out the window at Ajax Mountain— Ajax towering high over the town like an 11,000-foot giant frozen tsunami about to crash down on the town, and coming down it were all these little gods and goddesses like toy soldiers with white rooster tails shooting out of their ski boots. I said, "Ramona, we must go up and see the gods and goddesses come down. Let's try to get closer to this giant. Let's go up on the gondola and see what we can see."

So up we go on the Silver Queen gondola—we're the only ones on the gondola not in ski outfits and without skis, and the whole thing was swaying in the wind.

We stagger out snow-blind into waist-deep snow, which we are both breaking through up to the knees. Me with my SoHo greatcoat on, with its collar turned up, my black wool dockworker's hat from Canal Street. Ramona is dressed in black, with a Persian-lamb hat. She looks as if she just came over the Berlin Wall. And we're busting through the snow—up to our knees in it—when suddenly I see that I'm up there with my people, all of them, up there: Cheddy, Chip, Puffy, Muffy, Babs, Sis, Jib, all of them—my people, who all had that inner cheerleader voice in them. Someone told them to go for it and they did. They went for it and won! They all passed geometry, passed algebra, passed trigonometry, passed calculus, went to Phillips Andover Academy and on to Harvard, Brown, Yale, Dartmouth Business School, and they are all up there and they are skiing with three children—they're skiing. Looking like Easter eggs, very expensive Easter eggs. My people mixed in with *People* magazine—Ivana, Sharon, Arnold, Dustin, Faye. They're there, and they're having a good time! They're having a good time in the day. It's like a party in the day, they're having fun! And the kids—the kids are going over the white edge of the world: It's just this whoa—you see them go shoot! I think they're disappearing. I think they're shooting straight down the slope. I had no idea about traversing the slope, and we're up there—and the view! "Oh my God, Ramona, I've never seen anything like this. Look at the view!" I've never seen so many theres. I could be there, I could be there, I could be there—oh my God, the sudden partial gratification of omnipotent ubiquity! Yes! And I caught a very bad head cold. And we downloaded on the Silver Queen, me thinking, Why would these people—why would these little gods and goddesses come to hear me perform my monologue *Monster in a Box* at the Wheeler Opera House? Why would they come to hear my neurotic, ironic, hypochondriacal non-athletic voice perform a monologue about me, a man who can't write a book about a man who can't take a vacation?

I tried to wipe that white Garden of Eden out of my mind. We moved on with *Monster in a Box* and toured it across the United States—opened at Lincoln Center, to successful reviews. Then the book, the film, the video, the void. Over. Finished. What now? Another monologue? What else? There was always a new crisis, a new life drama to talk about. I only hoped I wasn't creating them just for material. I was losing my sight in my left eye. I hoped I wasn't bringing that on myself just for a story. But it was great material for a monologue— so I started working on it and called it *Gray's Anatomy*. I was building it not unlike I'm building this one.

I was traveling across the United States with Ramona again—we were in Scottsdale, Arizona, and I was very tired of being on the road, being in what I called "a windowless art house," all the time sitting at a table recollecting my life. I found that I wanted to be more involved in the present, more active. I wanted to do something extremely physically exertive, without an audience, to do something that wasn't going to be a story. I wanted to exhaust myself. Spend myself to the point where no story would be left. I wanted to burn. I wanted to climb down to the bottom of the Grand Canyon and climb back up in a day. I thought that might do it. That's how I was going to get in touch with my body. So the plan was, when we finished with Scottsdale, we would go up to Flagstaff to stay overnight with an old friend of mine and in the morning we'd head off to the Grand Canyon.

The following morning, while having breakfast in my friend's kitchen, I looked out the window and pow! There they were again! Those glistening white fingers, this time the San Francisco mountain peaks! "My God, David, you live at the base of a ski slope! Look at this. Look, Ramona. Let's go see the gods and goddesses come down, just once, before we go to the Grand Canyon."

So on the way to the Grand Canyon we go up to the slope, and Ramona sees a sign for ski lessons, and I say, No, no, no, I think I just like watching. I really do, I mean you'd have to have a death wish to do this, and if you did, it could be dangerous.

So off we go to the Grand Canyon. It's a beautiful

spring day, although it's rather icy and slushy. I have crampons on. We're starting down the Bright Angel Trail and I suddenly realize, Hey, wait a minute, the Grand Canyon is really an upside-down mountain! It's a very large, inverted mountain. It's a depression, it's a very big depression. And as I went farther down into it I became more and more depressed. Going into the shadow, I cried, "Light!!!! Light, Ramona! Give me light!!!! Let's go back and take the lesson."

We go back to David's house and he's a little confused, like what's happening with Spuddy Gray, my old friend, he's so—vacillating. One minute he's here, he's gone, he comes back. Well, they're putting up with it. After all, we're going to stay only one more night. Also, they were planning to close the house down the following day because they were going south. For a vacation. Which felt weird to me, because where they lived felt like a vacation.

Next morning, couldn't be more beautiful, not a cloud in the sky. After breakfast Ramona and I sign up for the lesson. For forty dollars you get equipment, a lesson, and a lift ticket for the day. So we are waiting there for our ski professor to come out and I realize as I stand there in the snow that it is not so much the skiing I'm afraid of but the lesson. Because I have never learned anything in my life. I mean, I'm one of those who is perpetually getting lost. I stop at the service station for directions and they want to draw me a map. I say, Please, no maps. It's like a bad geometry class. Sausalito, Isosceles, whatever. Just give me visuals, please: turn left at the purple house, right at McDonald's, straight at the live-oak tree. I couldn't get up on water skis, although I'd tried forty times. I never made anything from a recipe in my life, I just tossed it all together. When I was a kid making a model airplane, I'd make a big gluey ball with wings coming out of it.

In eighth grade I had to do a science project—I wanted to make a ham radio because I loved to listen to the hams talking, but I couldn't follow the directions, so my next-door neighbor did it for me. I got an A, or he got an A vicariously. I could never take it home— I'd be in homeroom and I'd look at the radio on the shelf and I'd think, That's my radio, I should take it home and listen to it. I never did. I would procrastinate, I think, because of the shame I felt for not having built it. Someone else finally took it home. To their home.

When I was fifteen I thought I had to rebuild my engine. Everyone was rebuilding their engines at fifteen. I didn't have an engine to rebuild, so I bought a '40 Ford coupe, and took the engine out and brought it down into the basement and tore the entire engine apart. My father paid $35 to have the body of the car towed out of the yard.

So we're standing on the slope, and out comes our

ski instructor. He begins by telling us that he's a retired heart surgeon. And now he's doing what he always wanted to do, being a ski instructor. He tells us that we could not be in a more beautiful spot. We're standing on 150 inches of packed powder looking over the rim of the Grand Canyon. Indeed, it was beautiful.

We begin the lesson, and I have to say, it was vaguely reminiscent of geometry, starting with the snowplow. What a freakish thing that was. The skis turned in as I tried to get my balance, doing the old caveman crunch. Ramona was doing very well, the whole class was doing very well; they were beginning to learn to turn. Snowplow turn to the right, the left, the right. But for some reason I could traverse only to the left. Of the whole class only I couldn't turn right. I did a beautiful left traverse, though. Then I'd snowplow down, take the rope, tow up, and traverse left. "Hey left, hey look at the left!" Left, left, obsessively left. I could not get around—I thought that I had to think my way around into a right turn. I didn't understand how to get around.

Now everybody had gone in and Ramona was on the porch waving me in, saying, "Time to go back, Spald! Gotta catch the plane to Newark!"

"Ramona, I can't go, I have to turn right."

"Spald, please, there'll be another time."

"How do you know, how can you say that? How do we ever know?"

I'm in the car, Ramona is driving. I'm down, I'm way

down, I'm like a four-year-old who doesn't want to go to preschool. You would not have wanted to be there. We get to the airport, I've got my head down, we're checking the bags, and all of a sudden, before my bag is on the conveyor belt—they're weighing it—I flip out. And I yell, "No, no, I can't go! I have to turn right! I have to turn right on skis. I've got to call David to see if I can stay at his house."

"No," Ramona says. "You can't call them, they're closing up the house, remember. They're going away on vacation."

Meanwhile, the woman checking the bags wants to know: "Are you flying with us or not?"

"I can't. Wait, I—wait a minute, ma'am, before you check my bags on. I was up at that slope in Flagstaff and I didn't turn right. Is there a ski lodge up there I can check into? I have to take another lesson."

And she says, "Mr. Gray, I am here to check you on the flight to Newark. I am not a travel agent. Now, if you want to use the telephone before you . . . I think there's someone here who should not be flying with us to Newark today."

Ramona has got me over in the corner, saying, "Spald, what is wrong with you?"

And I say, "Ramona, I am tired of being a VICARIAN. I want to live a life, not tell it! I want to turn right on skis!"

And Ramona says, "That's it, it's time for a little crisis

intervention. I'm calling your brother Rocky in St. Louis."

She calls my older brother in St. Louis and says, "Hi, Rock. You gotta help out. Spald's in the Phoenix airport and he won't get on the plane because he can't turn right on skis."

He says, "Put him on."

And I say, "Hi, Rock. Listen. I'm out here in Arizona and all day I've been turning left and I love it, but I wanna turn right, and I wanna stay. I don't know what to do."

Rocky says, "Hmm. Well, don't you have a difficult life. You know what you should do, Spud, I think you should fly back with Ramona to New York City, and then go up to New England and learn to ski with your people. I mean, really, if you can learn to ski in New England, you can ski anywhere."

"Oh really, I never heard that jingle before."

And with that little jingle in mind—If you can learn to ski in New England, you can ski anywhere—I flew back to New York City.

I get back, I call up Vermont and for some reason they have no snow. They don't understand it. They were supposed to have snow. Back then, I thought it was global warming. After this year I'd say it was weather psychosis. I think the weather is now imitating us. Nature is imitating us, and it's FUCKED! Have you noticed how in denial these television weather people are? In New York City they are, anyway: "Hi, everyone! We've just had three straight days of 70-degree temperatures in February, Los Angeles has nothing on us!" As though this was something to be desired! This nuclear weather!!!

And I'm back in New York, and I'm in a funk—renting ski videos, I'm so desperate. What a bore! They're like porn films. Similar exhibitionist gymnastics, similar music, similar vicarious feeling provoked in you: that old, I-wish-I-was-in-the-center-of-all-that lonely feeling. I don't know what to do. My friends are giving me advice, some are saying that I should go into classical psychoanalysis. They say, "Sometimes a ski is not a ski." Others are recommending Prozac, and the ones I trust are saying, "Spald, you've worked very hard. Perhaps too hard. You really should take some of your savings, take some time off, and go learn to ski. You only live once."

So that was why I didn't want to get on that plane in Phoenix. I was stuck back in New York City. Damnit all, once you enter, it's so hard to get out! It takes so long to get to the airport! It's a soul-killing daylong drive to get to the airport, and once you get there, then you have to fly!

I'm falling into my New York habits, just getting into the routine of it again, and not able to get out and break the inertia. What would an average day be like back then? Oh, I'd wake up when I'd wake up, usually after seven hours' sleep, 7:30, 8:00. Then I take my morning pee, and as I am peeing, I hear that little old voice in my head, every morning, say, "Remember, you are going to die." Imagine, I forgot that for seven hours. This usually causes an erection and I have very anxious sex with Ramona to try to work off the anxiety of death, and then after lying there in a stupefied heap of petite morte, I talk about my dreams, or maybe get out the *Mayo Clinic Family Health Book* to see if I have any symptoms of disease. I mean, there are 2,740 diseases in that book, how could I not have one? Then I do my yoga stretches, have some breakfast, some coffee, write in my journal. But what would I write? Maybe something like I'm telling you now. Then I'd go to my little bookshelf and take out a book for morning reading, maybe *Becker's Denial of Death*, underlined profusely in red, and read:

> *The irony of man's condition is that the deepest need is to be free of the anxiety of death and annihilation —but it is life itself that awakens this anxiety, and so we shrink from being fully alive.*

Closing the book, I go out for a walk in New York City to try to be fully alive. I'm not interested in buying anything anymore, I don't look in shop windows, I'm tired of the architecture, I'm searching for a park. I don't want to go up to Central Park because I don't want to ride on the subway, I want to walk to a park. So I walk to Washington Square Park. Basically a dysfunctional fountain with broken benches around it. And I walk around that fountain, obsessing on what I could do to feel more fully alive. Well, okay, so I'm obsessing on where I could go to turn right on skis, thinking about Kathie, a woman I had met on the road who had moved to New York and had sent me her phone number. Should I call her, should I "touch base" with her? Drop in for some tea? And I'm dwelling on the fact that I'm going to turn fifty-two years old, and I'm thinking about Mom, and how she committed suicide at fifty-two, and did that mean I was gonna do it, too?

Around that dysfunctional fountain I go, peeling the onion of my mind, running into the same Jamaican drug dealers each time around, trying to sell me the same drugs each time, not recognizing I'm the same person. Saying, "Hey, man, what's happening?"

"Hey, good question, what *is* happening?" I reply.

Then I go over to West Broadway to the Pita Cuisine and get one of those whole-wheat pitas stuffed with hummus, and if it's a nice day, I sit out on the deck thinking about turning right on skis, thinking about Kathie, about Mom, and then thinking, Oh, I'm so very fragmented today.

Then I realize I'm not fragmented, because there is

one whole witness part of me that is watching all this stuff. And I try to catch the whole part. Then I try to observe the part that's watching the whole part that's watching the fragmentations, and I try to observe the part that is observing the part that's observing the part —until a beautiful woman walks by and I am—*present!*

I go back to my loft and take the messages off my answering machine. Same old same old. Will you endorse my book? Have you read my filmscript? Will you do us a benefit? Then I put my yoga mat down and lie on the floor, a little afternoon respite, put on my stereo earphones, my little Walkman, and listen to my favorite afternoon spoken-word tape, Peter Coyote reading from *Zen Mind, Beginner's Mind:*

> *Transiency. The basic teaching of Buddhism is transiency or change. That everything changes is the basic truth for each existence. The cause of all suffering is the non-acceptance of this truth. Without accepting the fact that everything changes, we cannot find perfect composure.*

And off to sleep I go, waking up slightly anxious and depressed, in my small dark loft, no light, outside Canal Street traffic, graffiti on the walls, tarpaper on the building roof below, and cocktail hour! Get out the V-8, Tabasco, Worcestershire, horseradish, lemon, celery, Sky vodka. Mix and shake, turn on the news, *All Things Considered*, and wait for Ramona to come back from the office, where she has been working on her ongoing filmscript. That was my day. Back then. Before the big change came. Not such a bad day. But there were always those impingencies coming into my life, and I was always wondering, Was I creating them or were they just arising from the nature of reality?

Now, I knew I wasn't my mother, or at least my friends told me I wasn't. I had to be reminded! I knew I didn't have to go through what Mom went through. But that's not to say that somewhere in my "un" there wasn't some sort of program going on that I was going to join her. And the way it began to come up was in the form of suicide fantasies. I never felt I was creating the fantasies, they would come to me like a film. I knew they were fantasies, and I was attempting to embrace them and look at them without feeling as though I had to act on them. They were quite wild. I mean, they were way out there.

The first suicide fantasy took place in Ireland. When Ramona and I were traveling through Ireland, we went to see the Cliffs of Moher—I wanted to go because I thought it was spelled More and at the time I could not get enough. The Cliffs of Moher are these spectacular 400-foot-high rock cliffs, and Ramona and I were out on them alone at cocktail hour. I remember I was drinking a can of Guinness stout. Most of the tourists had gone home. There we were, looking out over an Irish sunset; you know, gray sky over gray sea, gray observed by Gray. And the thought occurred to me that what I wanted to do was a kind of Road Runner suicide, in which I would step back, take a running start, streak by Ramona— "Bye-bye, Ramona, *beep-beep!*"—and shoot off over the cliff, and just as I was about to drop down 400 feet, I would turn and see her face. And that last image on her face, that last distressed look, is what I would take with me to my watery grave. The thought of this fantasy made me cry. I could not stop crying, and I could not stop telling Ramona this fantasy, over and over and over again.

The next major suicide fantasy that started to take over my consciousness was when I was out on the road again with my monologues and I was alone in Taos, New Mexico. Out behind my hotel was a hot tub, and I had a fantasy. I would get myself a whole bunch of Quaaludes and a straight-edged razor. Then I'd eat the Quaaludes and get into this very hot water and, once I turned to rubber, just lightly draw the straight-edged razor across my wrist. Then I thought, Where would I ever find Quaaludes, in this day and age, and once I did and took them, I'd probably feel such an incredible state of well-being that I would not want to kill myself.

In the midst of these silly suicide fantasies, a very powerful, synchronistic event happened. Steven Soderbergh, the filmmaker who had directed *sex, lies, and videotape* and *Kafka*, approached me to be in his new film, *King of the Hill*. He told me he had only me in mind for this particular role, because he had read my novel, *Impossible Vacation*. In the novel, he said, my central character, Brewster North, is clearly ruled by regret. In his movie, Mr. Mungo, whom he wanted me to play, is ruled by regret to the extent that he kills himself.

I said, "Really! And how does he do that, Steven?"

"Well, right now I have him slitting his wrists."

"I'll do it!"

I really thought this was a very powerful and good opportunity to work out these fantasies in a creative way with a good director. So we started working on the film.

Now, if you haven't seen the film, you can certainly find it on video. It takes place in the Depression—the other one, 1929. It's about a young boy surviving the Depression by befriending all the people in this hotel he's living in, Mr. Mungo being one of them. One day the boy sees blood coming out from under Mungo's door, and there's Mr. Mungo, facedown in the sink, his wrists slit.

They are shooting the film in sequence and the last scene is the suicide scene, and it was becoming a very powerful event for me. I was deep into it and determined, once I finished, to celebrate in a wholesome, joyous way, which I had never known how to do up until then. I had always celebrated in a more dissipated Dionysian mode.

I had befriended my stand-in. I rarely speak to my stand-ins in films. Standing-in is an odd occupation. Stand-ins stand in for you while they adjust the lights, and then you come on and get filmed. So they're never on film; they're like nonexistent people. But on this particular film I had befriended my stand-in because he was a ski bum. His name was Barney, and what Barney did was take his stand-in money and pick up inexpensive flights on Reno Air. Bopping up there to Tahoe, skiing in all kinds of weather and seasons. He wanted to take me up there and teach me how to turn right! So I was hip to go, I just wanted to kill myself and get out of there.

We were into my last scene, the suicide scene, and I was in for makeup, which was extraordinary. It took two hours to build these slashes on the wrist, which actually looked like gashes, because they did it in relief. I had dried blood running down my hands, and with white powder all over my face, I looked white and ashen. I was outfitted in a white linen thirties suit with suspenders. Then they take me to my hotel room, where I have to lie facedown in the sink while they prepare the mix of blood and water to flow out onto the floor and under the door for the boy to discover. So not only is it a meditation on suicide, I also get to meditate for two hours on the mess that you leave for your loved ones after you kill yourself. I'm both dead and not dead, so I also get to see the face of the boy when he opens the door.

When we start filming the scene, I'm very excited because the plan is to get out of there as soon as I kill myself. Barney and I are gonna fly up to Tahoe, where I'm going to learn to turn right! Of course I'm always worried that the good stuff will never come, so I'm worried that there won't be any snow. Barney insists there will be snow, I'm going with it; it's early spring and I'm secretly praying for that glorious white stuff. So I finish my last scene and I'm ready to get out of there and Steven says, "No, there's another scene."

I say to Steven, "I'm dead, what's the scene? Resurrection?"

He says, "No, you have to be carried out on a stretcher, under the sheet."

I say, "You don't really need me on that stretcher if it's covered with a sheet. I mean, have my stand-in— no, my stand-in can't do it. Look, Steven, why don't you do it?"

He says, "What, Spalding, you don't want to be in my movie?"

"All right, if you put it that way. Look, I'll tell you what. It's gonna take you an hour to light the scene. Let me go back to my hotel right now, pick up my bags, and check out. Then Barney and I can leave for the airport right from the set and we'll make that Reno flight up to Tahoe."

I can't believe it, but he lets me go, with my wrists slit. I'm in the back of the teamster van to the hotel and I'm kinda flashing my bloody wrists at the driver, you know, kinda testing it out. He's just driving, he's in the rearview mirror, it's Hollywood, you know, just don't bleed on the car.

We get to the hotel, I'm checking out, and the woman looks at me and says, "How's the film going, Mr. Gray?" And I lift my wrists and smile, and she goes, "Oh, gross out. Should I leave your incidentals on your Amex card?"

I think, Am I not affecting anyone here? Does this not look real? And I think, I'm not going to leave this hotel until I have an effect on someone. Then this diabolical Halloween eleven-year-old-kid energy comes over me. I go into the pharmacy in the hotel and this —I was going to say older—woman was there—but she was my age actually. I say older because I felt like an eleven-year-old, and she reminded me of my mom. She was filling prescriptions, so she couldn't have been really like my mom, cause my mom was a Christian Scientist, but to some extent, something was going on there, and she was the only one in the drugstore.

I walked right over to her with my sleeves rolled up

and raised my arms and said, "Do you have anything for my wounds?!!!" And she said, "Oh my God! Oh! Oh! We have Mercurochrome!" Mercurochrome! I thought, That's ridiculous. She must be in shock.

And she ran off. She wasn't even looking for Band-Aids. She said, "Whatever did you do to yourself?"

I said, "Oh, I cut my wrist this morning." And then I realized I was trying to kill her. My God! I was acting this out in a big way, I was trying to reverse history. I was trying to show Mom what it was like for her if I were the suicide. Then I just apologized. I said, "I'm so sorry, I'm in a movie," and I ran.

I got back to the set and said, "Hey, Barney, let's get out of here. I'm starting to lose it, Hollywood's making me cuckoo! Let's go learn to turn right."

The other thing that was happening, and I had forgotten about this—it happens on every film and I just put it out of my mind—you know, you're working on a film, a fourteen-hour day or twelve-hour day, you just have blinders on, you don't look around. And just as you're on your last day, it's like lollipop day at school. The blinders come off and you're looking around for the first time and oh, I always spot the, oh, the oh ah—look at *that woman!* The most beautiful woman. She's never an actress, she's usually one of the production assistants. She's been there all the time, she's in her Bermuda shorts; I just hadn't looked her in the eyes before. And suddenly it's oh, Lord, sweet Lord. This woman's name was Donna Lane. Oh, Donna. Oh my God, oh, I've come home. Oh my God. Oh, I must, oh.

And I happened to catch her gaze. You see, I feel it's reciprocal, you understand, and I happened to catch her gaze when my face is down in the sink and I'm supposed to be dead. I looked over, across that trail of blood, at Donna's eyes. And I knew I had to be with this woman. How could anything that feels so good be bad? And at the same time I think of Barney and how I'm supposed to go with him—and I begin to think, Why? Why would I go off with a strange man to Tahoe? What if there's no snow? I could be tripping on magic mushrooms in the desert with Donna. What would happen if there was no snow? You see, I'd end up in a condo with this strange guy. I'd been in a ski condo before, it was like an architectural Bardo. But at the same time, I'm getting away, I'm pulling away and I'm going with Barney. This was really something new. We're going to catch that flight, although I'm seeing Donna's face projected on his face. I'm seeing Donna Lane's eyes projected on Barney's eyes. And we get up there, and I don't notice any snow in Reno. Barney assures me that there will be snow at higher altitudes.

So we rent a car and we're driving up to the condo. But Barney wants to stop at the state line to do a little gambling first. And I think, Oh, is he one of those? Is that why he's dragged me up here? He's not really a skier, he's a compulsive gambler and he won't admit it. I'm so bored with it, I go in and it's like a windowless shoebox. I'm bored playing red, black, odd, even, taking no big chances. Barney is drawn to the slot machines. We go in to the slot machines. There's this woman who's just winning like crazy, and the money is pouring down, and she's chain-smoking. She looks evil. She's got these horn-rimmed glasses on, with costume jewelry, and she's winning, like evil forces often do. Barney is looking at her and drooling, and she looks up and says, "I bet you want my machine!!!" And I, standing straight as a Boy Scout, say, "No, we're skiers! We've really come up here to ski!" And she says, "Well, hang it up, my daughter's up here to ski, she was out today, and she said there's nothing but rock, grass, and stone."

I say, "Ohh nooh. Oh, Donna . . . Oh, Barney . . . Oh, Donna . . . Oh, Barney . . . Oh oh oh . . . what are we going to do, Barney? Do you believe in a snow god?"

"Spald, if there was a snow god, I would have it hanging around my neck. Do you think the American Indians prayed for snow?"

We left the casino and walked outside. It was ten o'clock at night and it was snowing! Oh, blessed snow! It was a great big Sierra dump. It was as if I picked up my old glass paperweight snow dome and shook it hard.

We're driving back to the condo and I am blissed. I

can't sleep. I'm like a little kid at Christmas. I'm like a fireman. Lay it out! Lay out all this stuff! I've never been out of my loft before noon, and we're going to get out early! We're gonna do it! We are gonna make tracks. We are gonna turn right. Put the boots out to keep them warm, all right. Lay it all out, Barney. Lay it all out for a quick start.

I could barely sleep. I was up before dawn, pacing back and forth. It's still dark out but it's snowing, it's still snowing! Barney!!! Wake up, get the Chap Stick! Get the vitamin C, get the echinacea, get the oranges, get the goggles. I get it all together, I get my stuff on, okay; I get the coffee going, uh-huh. I get on the thermal socks, thermal underwear, more coffee, thermal tops, more coffee—hurry—bibs up and buckled, down vest on. No. Take your down vest off, put your turtleneck sweater on, put your down vest on, more coffee—oops, gotta take a shit! Oh, take off the shell, the vest, the turtleneck, and pull the bibs down; then put all back on: grab hat, baklava, poles, gloves, skis—we're off! And we're driving, as fast as we can, to Barney's favorite PC beautiful slope. Oh, what a day! Oh my God, we're off to Alpine Meadow. He loves it there, because he says there are no snowboarders; there is hot broccoli soup, you don't even have to microwave it; and there is classical music on metal speakers, not rock and roll, when you come down at the end of the day. And there's an "adaptive" ski school.

We arrive to find locals already lined up, they haven't even opened the lifts yet. They have Day-Glo tape stretched across the gate, and Booooom!!! Booooom!!! Dynamite, we hear dynamite in the distance, dynamite to break up the avalanches, rumbles and echoes against Sierra granite cliffs, and we feel the rumble. We feel the rumble in our chests and all around our hearts far below the snow-peaked mountains, and all the locals cry, "Hey, awesome, man! awesome! rock 'n' roll, phat snow, phat snow whooo, high five, man." And it is phat snow, I mean the mountain was skinny the day before. Now it has a great white belly, and hey, there's fresh powder there. There are runs they can do—they can do unmarked powder—make fresh tracks in the trees, and they can free ski out in the powder. The powder hounds are there—all panting like dogs on their phat skis. And I'm gonna turn right!

The Day-Glo tape is pulled and we get on the chairlift. I ride up with Barney. We start down the blue slope, the intermediate run; I'm trying to emulate him. I'm behind him, damnit, and I'm going left, only left into the bushes. Coming out the other side with branches in my mouth, like a Botticelli. I say, That's it, I'm not hanging you up anymore. I'm going over to the bunny slope. I'm going over to the meadow to try and do it on my own.

When I got there, I realized I was skiing right in the middle of the adaptive ski school. I was in with the handicapped, and it felt just right and also incredibly inspirational. I saw quadriplegics being lifted out of wheelchairs and put in little gondolas that looked like motorcycle sidecars that had little ski poles with foot-long skis attached to them. Oh my God, Spalding, if you can't learn to turn right on this slope you better hang it up. And I begin, and damnit, I can't think my way around into the right turn. I crash. I get up and I crash again. What I'm amazed by is how my body survives these crashes. Yard sales all over the place, and yet I'm up. No inner cheerleader's voice, but I'm back at it. And I'm down, then I'm up again, and then all of a sudden it happens.

It was ineffable—there's no other way to describe it —it was just—it happened—as though it did it, to me. I had not had the experience since 1946, when I had first learned how to pump on a swing on Thanksgiving Day. A simple shift of weight and suddenly I turned right, then left, and right again, and left, and—boom. I was down. What happened, what was that? Get up immediately, do it again. Oh, it's happening! Boom, crash, down. People ski by me and fall. I crash, I'm in such empathy. Or if I'm skiing, and I think, Oh my God, Spalding, you're skiing!!! Crash. I'm down again.

Then I'm up again and I feel something. It's a brand-new feeling. I'm in balance. I'm in the zone. All my life I've felt sort of out of balance with everything. Now I was balanced on skis, but it was such a very new and precarious balance that the slightest incident would throw me off. Some excellent skier would ski by me and I'd be stolen away from my center. He's so much better than I could ever be, and crash, I'm down. But during those rare moments when I'm up in balance, I feel hints of perfection. It's like Zen, but not as subtle. I also had a shocking insight, which when I had it made me fall, and that was that all my life up to this point I had been committing a subtle form of suicide. I would never wholly occupy the place I was in. I would always absent myself in some way by thinking, Oh, this almost feels all right but I could be there or somewhere else, so I was always a little bit not present. And now there was no room for that. If I was not whole and completely there and balanced on my skis, I would be DOWN! The mountain would HIT me hard.

And I love it, as I go down again. But I'm up, and hey, it's time for lunch.

I join Barney and tell him the good news. He says, "Great. Far-out. Awesome. Right on," and he invites me to ski with him.

Now it's packed powder all the way down, and it is a "to die for" day. To die, beautiful. It reminded me of the illustrations in the Thornton Burgess West Wind stories my father used to read to us. You'd see Old Mister West Wind all anthropomorphosed. The great billowing cloud has turned into a face that's puffing and blowing. The wind shoots out of his lips upon the place below and we are below, Barney and I are below in that spectacular land of snow. We are below looking up at ribbons of little white snow flurries being spat from the mouths of clouds, and then the clouds pass, giving way to that glorious California sun. Vivid high-Sierra sun that highlights all the carved-out snow furrows made by the skiers who had gone before us. And we were hopping through them. We were hip-hop-hopping through the furrows. We were dancing in the light. We were dancing in the day. And yippee—hee-ha, all the elements agreed! Race, race to get another run! Get the last run!

"Oh my," said Barney.

"Look, look, they're chaining the lift chairs. No, no, please . . ." They had to restrain me: I was trying to bribe the lift operator.

"Spald, Spald, take it easy," Barney said. "We've been skiing for seven hours."

I'd never done anything for seven hours in my life except sleep. Seven hours, without thinking of death once. Ah, man. I was flatlining. Barney drove us back to the condo, where we unwound in front of a gas log. Watched the weather channel, whatever. Then deep, deep, dreamless oblivion-sleep.

The following day I woke up, and I thought, Now, there's skiing and there's life. And I don't want to live anymore, I want to ski. I don't want to come down off this mountain. I've never felt such a desire, such a sense of a mission, in my life. To just stay up on the mountain, to ski my way back to New England. Over the mountains of America. I saw myself like the central character in the John Cheever story "The Swimmer"—remember? Burt Lancaster was in the film. He swims his way through back-yard pools to his deserted house. Well, I'm going to ski my way across America, and I'm going to use my monologues as a vehicle—to get performance bookings near ski areas.

So that's the plan: I'm going out on tour with my monologue *Gray's Anatomy*, and the first great booking that I get is important to me because it's Aspen and that means I get a chance to ski the monster, Big Daddy Ajax. And I arrive—it's this great deal: they're giving me a condo, free ski lessons, a ski pass, ski rentals, and a little money. And I have to do just two performances. Now, there are two main mountains there: Ajax, the big daddy; and beside it, Buttermilk, lying like an elegant reclining lady—you can ski over her breasts and thighs —and then go over and get beat up by the "father" at the end of the day. The tickets are interchangeable.

So my plan is to take my lesson at Buttermilk and, if I do well, go on over to Ajax the following day. I've rented little 160's—those little stubbies, so I can turn easily—and I've got my free lift ticket. I'm waiting for my ski teacher, and while I'm waiting, I'm nervously reading the back of my ski ticket, which I'll never do again.

Skiing is an inherently dangerous sport which can result in personal injury, including catastrophic injury, death, or property damage. [God forbid property damage.] If you are not willing to assume the risks set forth in this warning, please do not ski in this area.

Sign, sign, sign, sign everything. Sign my life away and wait for my ski professor to come.

He arrives dressed like an egg with wraparound reflective sunglasses, and he says, "Hi, guy. Okay, let's begin. Sterling? Shall I call you Sterling? Hey, Sterling, do you want to hear a joke before we begin?"

"Okay."

"You know the difference between a vacuum cleaner and a snowboard?"

"No."

"Depends on where you attach the dirtbag.

"Okay. Slight bend in the knees, corresponding bend in the hips . . . good. Crouch and lift at the same time. Parallel skis, make them flat and parallel in the snow, slightly edged. Right. Using turns at the end of each traverse, we can proceed down the slope at any speed you so desire. Now weight forward, don't sit back, nothing natural about this posture, Sterling, nothing natural about it. Hey, hey—don't cave in! You're caving in your chest. Now, feet slightly apart, supporting your body weight evenly, eyes front, neck relaxed. That's good, don't look down at your tips. Flex your elbows slightly, weight on the balls of your feet. Please don't stick your butt out. Now, your basic traverse stance is often referred to as the 'banana.' All right? Now, 'banana' is leaning down the slope. Basically you're falling down the mountain, Sterling, you know what I mean? You're falling down. Now banana arching. Skin still on the banana. Think of your ski suit as a banana skin if that helps. Nothing natural about it, you're really falling down the mountain. Another snowboarder shoots between us. That little fuck. I can't wait until one of them hits me and I can cash in on his HMO and retire.

"Okay, parallel skis, upper ski is slightly out in front of the downhill ski. Shift your weight and lift the upper ski: let it lead out, facing down the fall line. Basically you are falling down the mountain. Okay, now I'm going to traverse on down the slope. You stay there and watch me and then follow."

I stood there like a frozen banana and went back to the Wheeler Opera House to perform my monologue, *Gray's Anatomy*. My ironic, neurotic, hypochondriacal voice made all the exhausted skiers laugh.

The following day I was determined to set skis on

Ajax even though my guidebook said beginners shouldn't even contemplate that mountain. On the way to Ajax, I was remembering my Greek history and Ajax, the hero of the Trojan War, who had hallucinated that a flock of sheep were warriors and then attacked the sheep. Afterward, because he was so humiliated by this event, he killed himself. That was Ajax.

The first thing I do when I arrive at the mountain is get a trail map. I try to choose the easiest trail by name, and I choose "Dipsy Doodle" and "Pussyfoot." I'm standing on "Dipsy Doodle," talking to myself: "Skis parallel and slightly apart. Slightly. Slightly would be . . . Slightly? Relax arms and flex elbows . . . Flex elbows? Why did I let him call me Sterling? Crouch and lift at the same time. Ninety percent of your weight on your downhill ski—90 percent . . . Think of yourself as a banana. Don't stick your butt out . . . What butt? Weight over the balls of your feet." Now, I never knew my feet had balls. I'd heard the expression, but I could never contact them. Basically I feel like a bad geometry class; I feel fragmented, not whole. The other skiers are shooting by me, annoyed by my standing there, and they're all doing that little Austrian *vedel*, that little tight-assed boots and skis together, hip-hop bunny hop like an automaton. When they see me stalled there talking to myself, they stick their noses up and say, "On your left." You're not allowed to crash on Ajax. If they see you down, they just look up in the air and pertly say, "On your left." When you go down on Buttermilk, people stop and say, "Can I help you, guy? Are you all right?" But on Ajax it's just "On your left."

But I'm starting to ski. I'm turning and I'm going down "Dipsy Doodle" and I'm turning left, right, left, and then CRASH! But I'm up again, right up, get the skis back on, cursing—actually I'm swearing—I'm angry at the mountain, I'm having a good reaction. I haven't found my inner cheerleader voice; there's no way yet I have anyone in me telling me I'm doing good. But at least I've lost that damn self-deprecating "You're shit, you're no good. You'll never do this" voice, because the mountain was beating me up so hard it replaced that voice. The mountain just whacked me down, but I got right back up again. And exhausted by that morning I suddenly experienced the Zen miracle: I was hungry without looking at my watch. Time to eat!

I didn't have to ski all the way down the mountain, there was a nice gourmet restaurant, Bonnie's, at the halfway point. I ski down, take off my skis, drive them into the snow with all the other skis. Oh, I'm a skier now. Clomp on down onto the deck, big boots clomping like a man on the moon, order a well-done hamburger to avoid E. coli, and sit out in the sun, give over, relax into the ineffable. Oh my God. What a view. I had to pinch myself. Could this be Spuddy Gray, great failure of Barrington, Rhode Island? Skiing in Aspen, Colorado? Hey, the fat lady hasn't sung yet. This is incredible. And you know what? I'm alone without feeling lonely. I think I'm coming back into my body. There's no mirror, there's no audience, there's no one watching me, no one to image me, that's probably why.

Uh-oh. I see three people coming toward me, they're smiling. They've seen my show last night, they've seen *Gray's Anatomy*, I know it, I can tell by the way they're smiling, like they think they know me. But I like them, they're local. The first woman is Maggie, she's got a sweatshirt that says I CAN REMEMBER WHEN SKIING WAS MORE DANGEROUS THAN SEX. Maggie's a mailwoman, a letter carrier, and she's on a long lunch break. And then there's Jake, her boyfriend, who's a contractor. And then Martha, who used to be on Ski Patrol on Aspen Mountain and had to quit because she had recurrent nightmares from having to peel people's faces off trees. Now she's a ski instructor for the blind; she teaches blind people to ski at Buttermilk, and she's got the day off, and she and Maggie and Jake all want to ski with me.

So I say, "Well, I'm honored, but I'm really not skiing, I'm just up here falling. I'm practicing my falls. I shouldn't even be on this mountain."

They laugh and say, "Come on, we've skied the mountain hundreds of times and we'd love to be able to do it with you." And Jake is giving me this line about "pack-skiing." He tells me that if I ski in a group I'll learn faster. He says, "That's how the Balinese dance masters teach their pupils, kinetically. They're dancing right beside them and they simply pick up on the kinetic rhythms of the master."

"All right, all right, I hear you, I hear you. I'll give it a try."

So we go to get our skis on, and for me it's always like learning how to walk again for the first time. My skis are crossing, they really do feel too long, and they're turning like semis. But I am keeping up with them, and I am also crashing, and they stop, smile, and laugh. They don't seem rushed in any way. The day seems timeless for them. And the mimic actor in me is able to do what Jake told me about. I'm able to fall into a kinetic imitation of him. If I get close enough to him, I actually take on his posture and body moves so that my skis are closer together and doing parallel turns. I was getting into his balanced speed. There was a magnet-like pull in which I would get too close to him and almost *become* him. It was a drive toward some sort of strange fusion. I'd almost crash into him, and then I'd have to get back to myself and there'd be no one home. And I'd crash. It was like having someone else build your ham radio for the science project.

And so we're skiing, and Maggie, devil that she is, is relighting and passing around a snuffed-out marijuana joint every time we're going up, asking, "Anybody want a smoke?" "Oh no," I say, "that stuff just makes me think too much. No, 'think' is the wrong word—I'd be a scholar if that was the case. I mean my gears grind, you know what I mean? It's obsessive-compulsive gear-grinding; it doesn't go anywhere. I mean, if I was dancing in a disco all night, I'd try it, then I could work it out." "Oh, Spalding," says Maggie, "skiing is like dancing in the day, like dancing in the light. Don't say no, just say maybe."

Next time around, Maggie and I are riding on a double lift and she passes it over, and I just take three deep inhales, and I *begin to think*! I think so much I forget to get off the lift. And it goes around and stops and the lift operator is smiling, yelling up to me, "Hey, guy! Having a good day? Hey! Rock 'n' roll!" They're helping me down, the skis are falling off, now they *really* feel too big, I can't get them back on. "They're too big," I'm saying. What the hell is this? Must be the marijuana that caused it. But in defense of the hemp, once I'm up again I notice that my hips are much looser. Not that you're supposed to have loose hips when you're skiing, but it feels good; it's working. And I'm skiing with Jake now and I'm really in empathy with him. Something about men, all of a sudden, and skiing—it's going great! I'm on the fearful edge of being happy.

We're at the top of the mountain, waiting for Martha

and Maggie to come up, and Jake says, "Spalding, I want to show you something."

And I think, Uh-oh. He wants to teach me something, and immediately I turn into a frozen banana.

He says, "No, no, no. Look, you're doing great turns. But you're sliding down the mountain when you come out of the turn, you're not edging. Watch me for a moment—just watch. I'm going to roll my skis in, all I'm doing is rolling the edge of the ski in toward the mountain."

Oh, what a difference an edge makes! Now I am skiing behind him and I am edging. And we are all skiing down "Ruthie's Run." This was the great vertical terrain I had been falling down before. Now I'm edging! I am skiing down it! And I've got it! I've got the motion! I'm falling but not crashing. I'm falling into my turns and I feel it. In order to be in control, you have to be out of control. For a second you have to be in a free fall, then you catch it, and you have to have a leap of faith and believe that you're going to turn.

It's the first leap of faith that I ever had in my life. I doubted *everything* up until that day. If I doubted I could turn right, I would fall. Leap of faith and I'm around.

Maggie is cutting across behind me with stereo earphones on, shouting, "Spalding, think of it as a white wall of death!"

But this doesn't throw me, I'm able to hold up and keep my balance, and I know that's how Maggie gets her kicks. She, too, is a drama queen; she wants me to do a monologue about this, and she wants to be in it.

We all have a lovely day skiing in a pack, and I never thought it would work so well, but it did, though it all ended too soon. They said, "Okay, Spalding, it's been great, but it's close to four o'clock and now we're going to ski the mountain and you have to download."

"*What?* I would *never* download."

And they said, "Oh no, Spalding, you're just beginning. You're tired, it's the end of the day, it's a long run, and there's only one way down Ajax from here: it's through Spa Gulch." They tell me that locals refer to Spa Gulch at the end of the day as the "Valley of the Shadow of Death." It's shadowy, it's icy, and there is a convergence of all trails, skiers coming from all sides. They tell me that Maggie blew her ACL's out in the Gulch last year—you could hear them sputter and pop like wet spaghetti all the way up the canyon. "You don't want that to happen to you, do you?"

"I want to run the mountain with you guys," I say.

"It's your choice . . ."

So I decide to get behind Martha, the ski instructor for the blind, and go down with her. She's like a sleek weasel on long skis. Oh, what a beautiful skier. And we start down and I'm keeping up with her and I'm very excited because this is a very long run.

Now we were exploring the whole terrain and coming into the rhythms of that giant. Before, we had just been doing runs at the top. Now I was experiencing the mountain as a whole body. My own body was heating up in relation to this mountain. My breath was coming into the rhythm of that giant. I was turned on. The late light played like earthly magic, cutting sharp and bright through the aspen trees, which looked like storybook elephant legs, and the elephants were all grazing.

That same late light created a field of rainbow prisms that spread below us, stopping at the shadow's edge that led to a deep, dark, evergreen woods. I could feel the big pull of the mountain all around me as I hurtled down behind Martha. I was still and centered and in motion at the same time. There was no time to linger anywhere, only to see and feel it as it came, and then to let it go, or not even that, because there was no letting go since there was no containment, no memory, only flow, and a spectacular evolution of view. I said a prayer to my right eye. Oh, thank you, thank you, right eye. Thank you for not acting like my left eye. Thank you for this glorious vision. I'm happy to be alive!

Then I could feel the way the mountain was beginning to narrow as we came into a place of no sun. The sun was winking and flashing across the icy peaks. And I could feel and see the convergence of the trails as skiers from all sides of the mountain made their last run into Spa Gulch. I could hear the proliferation of snowboarders shredding the crusty snow behind me. I could hear them coming up behind me like some great roaring snow beasts.

Now we were in the tunneling mouth of the Gulch, and I saw Martha just ahead of me in one sleek motion ski up the wall of the Gulch and, at its crest, hop around on her skis and shoot back down into the oncoming traffic; she turned up again, and this time I was behind her. Was I skiing, I wondered, or were the skis skiing me? And up I went behind her, now looking straight up at a cobalt-blue sky and a new moon with a vapor trail across it, and straight down I went into amber light, and then farther down into icy shadows and oncoming skiers. It was as though at that moment I felt totally protected. It was like being held by the hand of some great snow god. Then up again, Martha leading, with me behind in her sleek wake, and up and down and up again and around and around and down and out and—YES! Born out of the thighs of Ajax!

We all came to a great snow-spewing, skidding hockey stop.

And we are all smiling. Martha is smiling, Maggie is smiling, Jake is smiling, and I am smiling so much it hurts. And Jake comes over and gives me a big high five. My first.

And I say, "Thank you, thank you for running with me today."

I went to return my rented equipment and the guy said, "You should be dead or in the hospital," and I said, "Why? Did you hear I ran the Gulch?" and he said, "No, you stole some lawyer's 195's at lunch. He had a ski lesson he had to take on your stubby little 160's. He's looking for you, man. Also, you were skiing on the wrong bindings all day. You're lucky you didn't break your leg. You're blessed, man. You're fuckin' blessed."

And with his blessing I felt I'd been initiated by the snow gods that day. I'd skied Ajax, I'd moved up to 195's pretty quick, and I was ready to ski New England.

But at the bottom of the mountain things were far from in balance. I was finding my balance on the top of the mountain and leading an increasingly reckless life down below. I think that when a self-destructive force is re-directed away from the self and goes outward, it often destroys something outside. And for whatever reasons (probably never to be fully known), I was systematically trying to destroy my own long and complicated relation-ship with Ramona.

Ramona and I met seventeen years ago, back in the old days when people would often go to bed together on a first date, and we did. And Ramona, being somewhat nervous about it all, mixed the wrong drinks, and just as I got in bed with her, she said, "Excuse me, but I think I'm going to throw up," and I ran and grabbed a big cooking pot from the kitchen and held her while she filled it up. I was able to be very nurturing and I came to feel that holding Ramona while she threw up was the first real bond of our love, and I think that because of this, I tried to make her throw up for the rest of the relationship. Only then could I express my love. There was also a very powerful unconscious attraction between us. We had a strong case of arrested development going on just under the surface of our adult appearance, where there were two children who had never been seen or, rather, had been seen by their respective parents and then gobbled up. Now the sad remains of these children hung out inside our adult bodies like frightened kids peeking through the leaves.

Both Ramona's father and my mother had been seductive and invasive parents. They did not mirror well, did not establish healthy boundaries. They were great, greedy consumers of their children, and they both died at fifty-two, victims of self-destruction. I think the night Ramona and I met, the two kids inside us cried out for each other, and we came together initially to try to reparent the needy child inside us both. This intention was never really all that conscious. Then somewhere along the way these two children got real competitive and my little rages overpowered Ramona's inner kid and tried to turn the adult Ramona into a mother for my raging child. I mean, when Ramona and I were alone in a room together, it was never as if there were just two of us. It was more as if there was this whole crazy family there. There were Ramona and I as the two adults. There was the image of us that I have created in my monologues. Then there were the two internalized kids looking out, and over our shoulders the two drooling ghosts of our dead parents. And flapping above us the disembodied voices of our various therapists.

So it was a very complicated and volatile, dramatic relationship, and the closer I got to that crucial age of fifty-two, the hotter things got. The more my inner kid began to beat up on Ramona's. Also, for me, Ramona had always been a great and wonderful container and processor. I don't mean to make her sound like a modern kitchen, but she was a fine container and processor and I felt there was nothing too raw or chaotic that I could not drop in her lap to fix. I think Ramona was good at this because she had always acted as mediator and go-between, the one that worked to smooth the endlessly turbulent relationship between her father and her brother in her family.

Anyway, the relationship between Ramona and me was an extremely complicated one, and because of my growing success as autobiographic monologist, a lot of the complicated tensions that plunged below the surface were not dealt with—for instance, the idea of creating a family. I think Ramona and I were both terrified of having children. I know I was. I'm sure the child in me felt there was no room for another child, and the child in me was pretty much the dictator of my adult behavior. Also, we were both dealing with issues of infertility and neither of us felt driven to plunge into the most extreme methods of fertilization, like *in vitro*. Looking back, I think I was like a kind of lazy romantic who felt that if it did not come naturally and just happen, then I would just forget about it and let it go. At the time I didn't want children, I thought, because I didn't want to have to get in touch with my inner cop. I did not want to be a responsible disciplinarian. I thought I didn't want to say "No." I was really afraid of children because of what I had witnessed as their chaotic need.

I remember one Christmas when my younger brother and his wife came to visit Ramona and me with their two-year-old daughter. We were all up at my little retreat house about an hour and a half north of New York City. What a chaotic two days that was. Amanda, my two-year-old niece, was, I'm sure, a normal two-year-old, but watching her behavior was, for me, like seeing an insane person, a cute psychotic. I felt I was cured of any need for children after that visit. I remember what the house was like after my brother and his wife and child went home and Ramona left for the city and I was at last alone. I remember the incredible peace I felt when I went out for a long walk alone and as I walked I thought, and felt deeply, "Let this cup pass from my lips." I do not need to go through this initiation of chaos. I do not need to father a child. It was a great relief. That perception caused a great sense of freedom and lightness in me. I felt liberated from the need to procreate.

Then that same winter something else happened when I was out snowshoeing on the golf course. I found a little kitten someone had thrown out into the cold, and this little yellow tabby kitty was hopping through the snow crying, "Save me, save me! I won't make it through the night if you don't take me in. Save me!"

I took that little kitten in just to take care of it until I could find a new home, and I remember now, in a sad warm way, how excited Ramona was to get up in the morning and go down to see this kitten and what a new sense of purpose it gave her. It was, after all, new life in our home, and I remember how I could see the kitten bring out that nurturing spirit in Ramona, or should I say that I saw the way the kitten redirected all the nurturing energy Ramona had away from me. I was aware how a child could have and would have changed our lives, and I was afraid. I dragged my feet in fear.

What replaced family was my work and the audience. I was working most of the time, developing new monologues and taking them out on the road. Ramona got caught up in all that with me. At times I felt as if we were mesmerized moths flying at the flame of fame.

In hindsight I see how Ramona and I needed to have

separate lives before we had a child. Ramona had very
much wanted to write filmscripts, which she was doing
when we first met, but for various reasons she kept getting sucked into my needs. Over the years I needed her
more and more as a sort of mother/manager, nurse/con-
tainer for my bottomless anxieties, as well as being the
director of my work. And my work was going very well.
We were both riding high on the magic carpet . . . and
then there was a crash, a very big crash. My "un" came
up in a big way. I fell asleep at the wheel.

So the closer I got to turning fifty-two, the more I
began to fragment, and Ramona could not stay on top of
my chaos. She couldn't process what I had dropped in
her lap. I started to disintegrate and go into a number
of personalities. I'd say one of my personalities was that
of a two-year-old. I say two-year-old because I've just
had some recent encounters with a two-year-old and I'd
say I was acting just like him. There's one theory that
two-year-olds have the omnipotent fantasy that they can
devour their parents, absolutely destroy them, so they're
testing the parent all the time, hoping this fantasy is not
going to come true. In other words, they are looking for
an indestructible boundary. I was always testing Ramona,
and also because I was good at casting Ramona in my
monologue, I had become very good at casting her as a
mother.

The other fragmented personality behavior that was

coming down the line then was that of Mom at her maddest. You see, I had witnessed the two severe nervous breakdowns that Mom went through, the second one lasting for two years and ending in her suicide. She was fifty-two years old and I was twenty-six. Both the nervous breakdowns were manifested in wild unnatural behavior: tearing her hair out, picking at her ears until they bled, crying out to Jesus, singing Christian Science hymns out of tune.

I was only ten years old when she had the first breakdown, and because I was young and around it all the time I could not help but take it in and absorb a lot of it, only, as I got closer to fifty-two, to play it back or act it out in a kind of uncontrollable, obsessive reenactment of her. Perhaps a way to get closer to her. What complicated things even more was that because I'm an actor who plays himself, there's a hazy line between what my act is and what my authentic behavior is. So I did not know if I was acting crazy or really crazy, or both, which I think must be a form of madness right there. In short, I was deeply confused and alienated from what I felt and thought about anything.

I do remember now as I write this that a couple of years after Mom's first nervous breakdown, the one from which she was healed by Jesus, I got real excited about jazz and joined the Columbia Jazz Record Club, from which I would receive one exciting jazz LP per month, and I remember that one of my many favorite records was of a live Benny Goodman concert at Carnegie Hall. The particular cut I remember was "Sing Sing Sing," in which Gene Krupa performed an especially arousing drum solo. I remember once taking my record player out in the yard and putting that record on and just going wild in front of my friend Chip Anderson. I remember going into a place where I almost lost consciousness and my whole body felt as if it was turning into a writhing thing no longer in my control. Then after I came out of it, I saw Chip's concern. He said, "You were just pretending, right?"

No, I wasn't pretending. I was in a crazy, irrational place that was somehow sanctioned and protected by that music. After all, I could always turn to Chip and say, "Oh no, not me. The music made me do it." But I knew that somewhere in me I was working out Mom's great irrational spirit, which had entered into me like some wild thing. Many years after the Benny Goodman trance dance, I found myself at last in Bali and witnessed an authentic trance, or at least a culturally sanctioned trance dance. I saw grown men seem to go completely insane. Bouncing around like they were all having grand mal seizures. It took at least five men, not to subdue them, but to cradle and guide them, to hold them in a firm, mastering way until they came out of it. I will never forget the sad longing I felt because our culture can only sedate and medicate the wildness in us. I wanted to be that Balinese man so badly that I could not stand to be a spectator. It made me cry.

Now in New York City in 1991 I was reversing my history: Mom was no longer going mad, my inner kid was going mad and saying, "Hey, Mom! Hey, Ramona, look at this—look at what it looks like to go crazy." The craziness manifested itself in imitations of Mom's behavior, or my actually becoming like her.

I was beginning to act out. And I was acting out in public places, much the way Mom acted. I'd be muttering to myself and involuntarily shouting out, but no one really noticed that in New York City. I can remember screaming in the streets at night and hearing my scream picked up by other people who passed it on down the street for blocks and blocks. What started out as real panic was turned into a performance by the people. Mom let out with a few of these yelps in a Rhode Island supermarket and they put her in a straitjacket and gave her shock treatments. If Mom had lived in New York City, she'd still be alive today.

Another fragmented aspect of self was the performer. I could still go onstage and give a good performance with no problem. In fact, I welcomed the isolated protection of the stage. Telling a life was so much easier than living one. Although there were times that I'd be in the Mom Mode all the way up to the stage door, barking and twisting on my way to the theater, people in cars slowing down to say, "Hey, is that Spalding Gray rehearsing in the streets?"

Then there was the fourth major personality fragmentation, which I ended up calling the sixteen-year-old, because I was having what felt like a sixteen-year-old's affair with Kathie, whom I had met on the road and who had sent me letters and her phone number when she moved to New York for a new job. I did drop in to visit her and we had more than tea.

Also, it was odd because Kathie moved to Thomas Street in downtown Manhattan and I grew up next to Thomas Street in Barrington, Rhode Island, but I didn't have a girlfriend when I was sixteen because I dated my mom until I was twenty-three.

Having an affair was not uncommon for me, but I had them only out on the road. Affairs were a big part of why I liked going out. They were the most powerful means of nonverbal communication I've ever known, as well as being fun. I always felt that it was safe to have them if they were kept out there and never brought home. Ramona had a few affairs, but nowhere near as many as I did. I guess we had an unspoken agreement that it was all right to carry on if we (or mostly I) did not bring it back home.

So why did I break that unspoken rule? I don't know, but I think it had something to do with fusion. There,

I've said it, "fusion," the word that has a ring of popular psychobabble and at the same time is a profound truth.

My mom and I were fused, but she broke that fusion by killing herself. But before she did that, I had a plan to break the fusion by joining the merchant marine and shipping off to Bali. I had an image of myself returning from Bali with a big sack over my back filled with souvenir trinkets, stories, and dirty underwear, and there Mom would be at the gate with her arms open wide, welcoming her Spuddy boy with unconditional love. And I thought Ramona would also always be there at the gate waiting for her man to come back from the Big See.

The fusion between Ramona and me over the years became very intense. I think that one definition of love is being able to see and accept the other for all of what they are. When we first met and were going around together, I saw Ramona and I loved her, but as she got closer, she became more like a mirror. We became like this unit. Like all units, at times it was exquisitely functional and at other times it was dysfunctional. What I'm telling you now is of course all hindsight. Neither of us saw it or dealt with it then, I think because we were on such a roll with my celebrity. My career as a monologist was going so well that we both got caught up in plugging ourselves into my image. It was as though my image was our child. That was the third point outside of us. My success was a drug and I was in a habit I was too addicted to stop. All my early life I was told that I was good for nothing, I could do nothing, would most likely not succeed at anything. So when producers and presenters began to offer me fees for the way I told the story of my life . . . well, you have to understand, I thought I had died and gone to heaven. I mean, I had to pinch myself. I was thinking, There has to be some mistake. Everyone is going to wake up tomorrow and not remember that they ever liked my one-man show.

I always expected that one day all the people that were booking me in theaters as well as the audience would say, "Well, enough of that guy's story. On to the next." And I was sure that there was nothing else I could do and I'd be out on the street. So I just kept taking all the work I could get, and Ramona, who probably shared similar fears, supported me in that.

For me the roll I was on became the roll "we" were on, and I got so caught in my image that I didn't know how to get back. There was no substantial self, no private self left to come back to. Both Ramona and I were living in this floating bubble, the public persona of Spalding Gray.

I think that the affair with Kathie was a break from this great rolling bubble of fusion. First of all, it seemed less complicated, not only because it was an affair, but because Kathie was less complicated, perhaps because she came from a not-so-dysfunctional family I didn't know.

Kathie was nowhere near as complicated, nor did she engage me in complicated ways. Of course, I understood I was only having an affair. It was in no way an in-depth relationship.

I thought we had a clear understanding that I was with Ramona for life and was just having a fun fling with Kathie. She said she wanted nothing more. Kathie seemed very independent and certain of herself. Also, she was a mother, so she had her hands full raising Marissa, her six-year-old daughter. This was important for me, because she had no leftover mothering energy to direct toward me, because if I get a whiff of that mothering energy, I just suck it dry.

Another difference with Kathie was that she was a real outdoors woman. She had grown up in upstate New York and had gone on camping trips with her family as well as having learned to ski in the Adirondacks at an early age. So we would often go for hikes in the woods just north of New York City. And once we took a camping trip, where we got to know each other a little too well for my comfort.

There was one other thing that happened with Kathie that had never happened with me and a woman before. I had been in what I think of as two long rela-

tionships with two different women, and I do not remember laughing with them once. I made them laugh a
lot, but we never laughed together, and that used to
really bother me. I mean, I had reached a point where
if I could have, I would have exchanged sex for laughter.
But I was laughing with Kathie . . . not a whole lot,
maybe six times in the two years I'd been seeing her,
and I was having very good sex, so it became an enjoy-
able situation I was reluctant to give up. With the con-
stant realization of how short life is and how I could die
any day, I was very reluctant to give up a situation that
was giving me so much enjoyment.

Now, things really started to heat up the closer I got
to the big crisis year of fifty-two, and to complicate
things even more, it was around that time that Ramona
re-expressed her desire to get married, and I felt that I
should be able to give that to her as a gift. I also thought
that once I married her, it would put an end to the affair
with Kathie. But at the same time I was so nervous about
it all, I had to propose to Ramona in front of my therapist, who knew I was having an affair with Kathie and
said nothing about that.

So Ramona and I made plans to get married. We both
wanted to get married on the beach near the end of
Long Island. In order to do that we had to go out early,
before the season began, to rent a house. We drove out
together to stay at a friend's and look for a summer

rental, and while we were there I had a very cryptic dream. I will never forget it. (Note to the dream: when my mother killed herself, my father had her cremated and scattered her ashes over Narragansett Bay.)

In the dream I'd been lying on a pile of ashes. My body was drifting down into the ashes and the ashes were coming up into my body—there was no boundary. And I thought, Ashes? What were they shaped like? The answer immediately came: "A sleeping bag." And I thought, But what do you mean, a sleeping bag? The answer was "You know, a mummy bag."

Then I thought, Oh, that's just a dream, and I got married anyway.

When I got married it was like a cork going into a glass bottle, and I started feeling, Oh, help, I can't breathe, let me out. The affair with Kathie heated up. Oh, I thought it was just going to *stop*. I thought just by my getting married it would peter out. And when Kathie told me she was pregnant, I fell down on the floor and went into a fetal position. When I came out of it, I said, "Get rid of it."

She said, "It's my body. I will make the choice. If I have this child, I will raise it, but I really have to think about it."

And I said, "Well, while you're thinking, I'm out of here." And I got out.

I met with Kathie only one more time and that was

on the street to pass her money for an abortion, and I said, "Get rid of it."

And she said, "I'm still thinking."

I am thinking back now in my of course selective memory to my history of not having a child with Ramona. One of the first issues I remember was the issue of competition. That came before the children issue. I can remember when Ramona and I were first hanging out and I used to spend nights at her office/apartment. She lived in an office space in downtown Manhattan that had been partially converted into a living space. There were lots of windows, and the morning sun would often warm our breakfast table. It was very romantic, and we lived an exquisitely romantic life. It often felt like a perpetual honeymoon, even though we weren't married. We were both completely into each other . . . or . . . well, maybe not . . . Thinking back now, I may have been completely into the way in which she was slowly getting completely into me. It may have been one of those mirror situations early on. But I remember a Sunday morning when Ramona wanted to make lox and eggs. We went to one of the only open delis in the area to buy packaged lox, and on the way Ramona talked to me about how *she* wanted to be the central character in our relationship. She needed our relationship to be more focused on her and her needs.

There was no doubt in my mind that Ramona was a real character. I mean she often acted like a character in a movie or a play. She had a similar dramatic approach to her life as I did to mine. And Ramona could come up with some great one-liners about her life. Anyway, it was on that day that I clearly saw how similar we were and also how potentially competitive we were. But I didn't care then. I was just going along with what felt good, which was just being together, being in bed together, lolling on top of each other. But I do remember that one Sunday morning when she told me she wanted to be the center of our relationship as the first warning that we ultimately were doomed to compete in what might turn out to be an unhealthy way. Perhaps I should have taken more notice, because just before I met Ramona I'd come out of a relationship that was highly combative and competitive. I was in a twelve-year relationship with a woman before Ramona, and I remember how Liz and I used to play Monopoly together early on in the relationship, and if she was losing, she would suddenly just flip the whole Monopoly board up in the air causing the play money and little houses to fly everywhere. Further on in the relationship Liz and I tried to collaborate in creating theater and that put the relationship to the big test. When she, at my request, became my director, it was not unlike what happened when I married Ramona. It was the cork going in the bottle. I began having an affair, which helped lead to our separation, but I think we really came apart over competitive-aesthetic differences. She went on to develop what became her theater company, and I went out on the road with the form of theater I chose to develop, the autobiographic monologue.

Now back to children. Why have I diverged so from the child issue? I see now that there was a reluctance to have children because of the way we all, Liz, the woman prior to Ramona, and Ramona and I, were searching for an artistic voice. All three of us, desperately and not so desperately, were searching for a unique form of self-expression. So the issues of children and family were not primary. Granted, creative people have children, but the children often come after they have found their creative mode.

The issue of children in my relationship with Ramona was certainly more pressing than it was with Liz before Ramona. I do remember that Ramona asked me early on if I was open to having children, because she did not want to stay in the relationship if I was not. At the time I think I said I was not closed to the idea. After that, a latency period of about five years took place before the issue of a child—and I think I'm clear on that, that it was a child we were talking about and not "children"—surfaced again.

It then surfaced as what I can only call one of Ramona's campaigns, and Ramona had to be a kind of campaign cheerleader to get me going around that issue. I can be a real lazy, stubborn stick-in-the-mud, resisting any change as if it was death itself, which ultimately it is. I think, although I did not realize it then, I could not have a consciously planned child. So Ramona began to get me focused on the issues of fertility. She was sure she had major fertility problems and she suspected that I did as well. Since I had never made anyone pregnant, and Liz, whom I had broken up with earlier, had had her first child with another man shortly afterward, I was beginning to wonder.

So, at Ramona's request, I saw an Egyptian fertility doctor. All I could think at the time was Oh boy, what great material, leave it to Ramona to find an *Egyptian* fertility doctor straight from the Fertile Crescent.

If I remember right, his report on me was that I had a good sperm count but many of them were misshapen. I do recall that he suspected that a varicose vein in my right testicle was heating the sperm in a way that made me less fertile. He recommended that I no longer wear Jockey shorts. He thought the Jockey shorts were "bunching" me too much. Ramona bought me silk boxer shorts, but I didn't wear them. Was I rebelling? I don't know. Perhaps I was stuck in my old lazy "bunching" ways.

I remember, too, that Ramona went through one artificial insemination. She sent me off like a little kid, address in hand, to a place where you basically jerk off in a cup. Anyone that has been through this knows how ludicrous it is to sit in that waiting room with all these other men and watch them emerge one at a time from the bathroom with a little cup of sperm in hand, and then give it to the nurse. When my turn came to go into the bathroom, I had no sense of how I could or would be able to make myself ejaculate into that stamped little cup. There was nothing erotic about this institutional room where some guy had just pulled himself off moments before I went in. Not only that, but there were stacks of *Hustler* and *Playboy* all around. It was as if someone's mother had gone mad and wanted her son to get into masturbation *right away*! Also, how do you rush it? I mean, there was all this pressure to fill the cup. After all, there were four other guys and a nurse outside, all watching the door.

I could not get excited looking at those magazines. All those photos felt so used. I felt as if I was getting sloppy thirds. I mean, all I could think of was the hundreds of men that had fingered these pages. In the end, I had to take off all my clothes so I could at least experience the eroticism of a fully nude body, and then end up doing it in front of a mirror. That felt more real than those pawed-over photos.

I don't remember very clearly, but I think I brought my hermetically sealed sperm vial home with me, and then Ramona rushed off in the morning with it to get it injected into her. I remember lying alone in the bed, not really feeling anything except Well, at least this might make a great story.

Also, there was some talk about adoption. Again, Ramona's idea. We went to one adoption workshop at the Manhattan YMHA. We heard arduous stories about what various couples who were testifying there had to go through to adopt a child. What exhausting, extraordinary stories they were. I mean, they were putting me to sleep. I began to think that the bureaucratic pain these people went through was somehow, although less immediately biological, much more than a metaphor for the biological pain of childbirth.

Relative to me, Ramona was a realist. I think she had a better sense of what it would take to enter into the role of parent. I, never having been a fan of reality, thought about children and parenting in the most flamboyantly romantic terms. There were, in my imagination, two central images having to do with children. The first was my own version of *Catcher in the Rye*, only I am Holden Caulfield and I am naked on a cliff at the edge of a rye field, and I am catching all these naked children that come flying out of that rye field at me. I am catching them in my arms just before they go over, my arms all full of laughing naked children, and there are never enough. Another image I had was of me naked again; the children are eating me, only they have no teeth and my flesh is vanilla ice cream that regenerates as soon as it's eaten. Both fantasies had to do with me and the children. The mother was never there.

When I think back to that time when Ramona began to take fertility drugs, it seems to me that there was a lot of infertility around—that is, among Ramona's age group—and I remember discussing it with her, and we decided to draw the line at *in vitro*, or rather, she decided and I agreed. I really did not feel a pressing need for children.

After Kathie told me she was pregnant and after I passed her money on the street for an abortion, I went into a kind of denial. I played the old ostrich game, except my head was so deep in the sand it almost came out the other side of my world. I could have been living in China for the way I reacted. My body and head were in two different places. Because it was my body that made the baby and not my head, I had no "child thoughts," no rational reaction to parenting.

I could not find the right words or the right place to tell Ramona about Kathie's pregnancy, and keeping it a secret was making me more and more crazy. I was living such a false, divided life that I was beginning to lose touch with who I was or what I felt. I felt too many different ways to ever integrate them.

For as long as I had lived with Ramona, I had kept a journal, and I know there were times when she would take a sneaky peek. In fact, Ramona would find out about my secret private life often from my notes or journal entries. I'll give you an example in just a minute, but first let me tell something about the history of my affair with Kathie.

Kathie and I had been seeing each other in a rather loose, informal way for a couple of years before she moved to New York City in 1991, and I think we thought that the way we were carrying on was just fine and uncomplicated. She would often tell me that she knew Ramona and I would be together forever, for life, and I agreed with her.

If I was to have an "affair," which I knew I very much wanted, I thought Kathie was the perfect one and that she would be the one who broke it off when she decided she wanted a full-time man in her life. But then she didn't. She felt she had enough to do dealing with a new job and a young daughter to raise.

Back to Ramona reading my notes and my leaving the notes where they could be easily read. Once, after I had taken Kathie out to dinner, we went back to my place. After years of living in that loft together with Ramona, I still needed to think of it as "my place." (Ramona was in L.A. trying to make a film deal and I was so excited to be alone I couldn't stand it, so I had called Kathie.) What was that about? Back we came to "my place," and among all Ramona's and my personal things, including loving pictures of us together, Kathie and I had "hot sex." What were we thinking about, you might ask, as I am asking myself now. We weren't. That was the obliterating heat of it. The fantasy was everything, and the fantasy for me was about what I can only call the Land of Pure Sex. Sex without the complication of personality: body love. It was not unlike holy sex, but the reverse of what I call holy sex—the partners transcend each other's ego in the process of the act. In this case, I did not allow myself to fully know Kathie's ego, so it was so much easier to transform her into a good sex object. I have no problems with the idea of "sex object"; it's dangerous only when you don't know and love the person you're objectifying. In other words, when there is no deobjectivication involved.

What excited me was that I could objectify Kathie as well as myself and our bodies would become—I was going to say "timeless," but I really mean "historic."

Historic flesh. When I looked down away from Kathie's eyes, which I often did, and saw my erect cock sliding in and out of her vagina, I no longer saw Kathie or me; I saw the long, great history of human sex organs all doing their endless old in and out, and that was the place I had come to. I had not yet reached the realization that they could not stop doing the old in and out because they were part of a larger program of procreation. As for me, the more I objectified sex, the freer I felt. This splitting was not unlike what I did with my sex partner at college, followed by platonic weekend dates with Mom at home. When I had sex with someone I knew very well, it became claustrophobic and limited. In my fantasy with Kathie, we were prototypes, running the historic gamut from Adam and Eve to JFK and Marilyn Monroe. That is, the organs of. My erections became something quite outside me. My erections belonged to history. They were not mine. Perhaps the only experience that belonged to me in sex was my orgasm and my memory of it.

But I keep digressing. Am I trying to excuse myself? Am I asking myself how I could have brought Kathie into the bed I shared with Ramona? Or am I hearing you, the reader, ask that? I think what I'm saying is that because of the level of fantasy we were both in, the loft, my loft as I experienced it with Ramona, was not there. I don't know what Kathie experienced, because I did not ask her. I experienced only surfaces, contours, light. We never really lived in the loft. Ramona and I lived in it. Kathie and I lusted in it, and for selfish old me, that was all I thought I wanted. I may not have been happy, but I felt content, a certain animal contentment.

I gave no thought to the consequences, nor did my therapist, who encouraged my infidelities, saying among other things that the impulse to spread my seed around

was programmed in my DNA. To fight that was hope-
less. Just be careful with the force that drives all.

Ramona found out about Kathie's pregnancy not in
the way I had planned. We had moved back to our
rented house in Los Angeles. At the time, Ramona and
I were living a bicoastal life, and we had just moved
back to our little rented bungalow in Los Feliz. It was
there and then that I planned to take her out to the
desert to a resort called Two Bunch Palms and tell her.
I really had no idea how I would do it. It felt to me as
if I was taking her out there secretly to shove her behind
a rock. To just shove her and run.

But before I got a chance to do that, something else
happened, something that relates back to Ramona reading my notes and diaries.

After I had taken Kathie out to dinner and then
brought her back to "my loft," Ramona had found a note
the unconscious wanting-to-get-caught part of me had
left around by accident. It was a little 3×5 card on which
Kathie had scribbled a thank you note: "Thanks for the
dinner and the movie. Please throw this away as soon
as you read it." But I didn't throw it away. I turned it
over and used it as scrap paper to write a phone number
on. Two days later, Ramona asked for the number and I
said, "Oh, it's on that little card," and of course she
turned it over, read the note, and got very upset.

"Who is this woman?" she cried, and "Why am I not
enough for you?"

I kept trying to calm her. "Just an out-of-town pro-ducer. Nothing to worry about."

But why, I wondered, was Ramona *not* enough for me? I wanted her to be enough so very very badly, but it wasn't happening. At the time I didn't realize things don't just happen that way, you have to work work work all the time at making them happen.

So there was a subterranean communication that went on between Ramona and me, a communication of random notes and diaries left in conspicuous places, so it was no real surprise to me that Ramona learned about Kathie's pregnancy by way of a note. And what a direct and shocking note it was. Just after we got to Los An-geles, I wrote Kathie yet another card pleading with her to have an abortion. I didn't mail the card right away but instead hid it in a book I was reading called *The Philosophy of Sex*. Then that night I raved to Ramona about what a great book it was.

The following morning when I came back from ther-apy, Ramona was nowhere to be found. I couldn't under-stand her strange absence. I was disconcerted and unable to concentrate on anything. In fact, whenever Ramona was not present in our little house or even smaller loft, it was hard for me to feel centered, safe, or relaxed. After a while I sat down at my desk and tried to concentrate on reading a book I'd been writing. Then I saw Ramona's car pull up below my window and I got up to greet her. We had a small arched window in our door, so I caught a vivid framed look at Ramona's face just before she entered, and I was shocked to see the face that I had fantasized seeing when I had that Road Runner suicide fantasy of me jumping off the Cliffs of Moher in Ireland. I saw that terrible mixture of feelings: confusion, incredible giant concern, more drama than her great heart could contain, and for a second or more when she was having trouble with her doorkey, I saw my fantasy framed, the ultimate distress of someone I loved for being able to feel that distress so deeply. Then the door flew open and Ramona was full-blown and very real, and out it came.

"Did you make that woman pregnant?"

At last I let go with a sad, relieving "Yes."

What followed was two days of highly dramatic hysteria. I was rolling on the floor like an apologizing animal. "How can you forgive me. I know you can't." "That's right, I will never never never never forgive you!" Neither of us stopped crying for two days. It was a marathon of confused grief and despair, which ended with Ramona telling me that I was sicker and more fucked up than she had ever realized. Among other things, she said she was shocked and amazed by my apparent ability to carry on with this woman for two years behind her back without her perceiving it. I think Ramona felt that beyond being able to pull off my stage performance, I was not much good at organizing anything else in my life. So the fact that I could have pulled off so many clandestine meetings with Kathie amazed her.

Luckily for Ramona, she was able to have long phone sessions with her therapist to help her through this crisis. Her therapist at last came up with the final solution. Ramona and I were to fly back to New York City immediately and try to convince Kathie to have an abortion. "It would be," her therapist said, "like walking over hot coals." At the time I was in such shock that I didn't see how outrageous it was for a woman therapist to be advising a woman client to ask a woman four months pregnant to abort.

When we got to New York, Ramona and I saw Kathie separately. Ramona's session was brief. "That beady-eyed bitch. I don't think she's going to give an inch. See what you can do."

The following morning I met Kathie downtown in the Square Diner. I was not in good shape. I couldn't stop twitching and moaning. I couldn't catch my breath. I was in that old acting crazy or was crazy zone, and I pleaded with her to save my life by aborting the child. But I could see by the size of her stomach that all I said was ludicrous.

When we left the diner, I walked her to the corner and she said, "Goodbye, Spalding, and don't worry. I'll probably move up to Vermont and live with my sister. Vermont is a good place to raise a kid." At that moment

I felt she was right. I thought that would be a great place to visit a kid who could run like I did into the great joy of the outdoors.

Ramona and I both knew that Kathie would not capitulate, although we could not face it together.

Ramona said, "Death would be easier than this."

Over the months I became more and more disintegrated, to the point where I even lost my inner witness; I have no real narrative memory of the chaotic events that transpired.

I remember some bits and pieces. I remember trying to be kind to Ramona and telling her that it would all work out. And she for a brief time wanted to believe that. I remember her waking me in the middle of the night with the deepest sobs I have ever heard. I had heard nothing like them, nor do I want to again. Those cries came from the depths of Ramona's soul and poured out. I could only hold her, while I myself was dry-eyed. Then after the sobs subsided and I turned out the lights, she said, "You have broken my heart." And I knew I had. There was no doubt of it. I had, for whatever callous reasons, broken the heart of the woman I loved. I lay there like stiff, dry hair. I lay there in sleepless limbo hell. Our two separate hells lay side by side in the dark windowless room. Oh my God, that it had all come to this!

Out of all that hazy hell of disintegration, I can determine one date: September 27, 1992. I was at home, rather, at "my place." Ramona was at her office, but being too distracted to work, she called me to talk about something and we were interrupted by the call interrupt, which I took, and much to my dismay I heard this raspy voice say, "Good morning. This is Kathie's mom and I just want to tell you that you are the father of a beautiful baby boy."

I don't remember what my response was. I think it was a throwaway line like "Oh great, thanks for calling," and I went right back to Ramona, who immediately wanted to know who it was, to which I said, "Oh, wrong number."

When Ramona found out the child was born she requested that I not see him until there was some reconciliation between us and, once again, I went out on tour, this time to California. Touring my monologues had become a way to fly out of reality.

But on this tour, something unexpected happened. Whenever I took off in a plane to travel to another city, I was secretly glad that Kathie had gone ahead and had the child. I realized I'd been acting the way I did to try to preserve my relationship with Ramona. I felt I would die if I lost Ramona, and I remembered back to another time when I was stoned on grass in Aspen, skiing on Ajax. This was not a fun time, like the Spa Gulch run, because the marijuana did not lessen my anxiety but instead made me very uptight. Maybe it all had to do with the people I smoked with. Maggie, Martha, and Jake had been so much fun to be with that it made getting stoned fun. Then there was this other time when I did it with people who were not as open, and I slipped into such a dark fantasy that I couldn't ski. All I could do was think about a story I was sure I was caught in. I suddenly saw the whole world as a hell realm. I mean, imagine that, skiing at the top of a mountain in Colorado and feeling I was in hell. But there I was, and that was what it felt like. And I thought, All the world is hell, but we're assigned one soulmate whom we will find only when we open our hearts completely, and when we open our hearts to love, we will find that other, and then together the two of you will pass through the hell realm of earth and into a true marriage of spirit. And then on that bright white slope I was sure that some evil force—call it lust, greed, fear—had invaded my soul, led me astray from Ramona, my true soulmate, and that I was doomed to misery and madness and confusion. It was a very dark, paranoid vision. I knew if I stayed in it too long I'd go mad, but at last the marijuana wore off. After that, I thought I didn't ever want to smoke marijuana again. It is not a dependable ally. I needed comfort, not more madness in me. A Bloody Mary, maybe. Anything but a joint.

I went on tour again; I couldn't take what was going

on. As I said before, Ramona had asked me not to see the child, and I preferred to be out of the city so I wouldn't have to think about him. I was really thinking of jumping ship, I have to tell you. I was thinking of just getting away from the whole thing by jumping ship and going to live in California. I would move to California and become a vegetarian. But while I was out there on tour Ramona called and said she'd seen Kathie on the street with the baby and it had destroyed her. She'd gone to bed. Would I please come home? I went into another paralysis. I was paralyzed and divided. In my imagination I saw myself sitting on the bed comforting Ramona. And I also saw myself standing beside Kathie, meeting my son for the first time. For two days I was quite paralyzed. And for two days I was quite out of my mind, lying on the floor in a stupefied trance.

Then a couple of friends who had been paying close attention to my erratic behavior felt it was time to get me on a plane back to New York. They helped me get dressed. They helped me find my airplane ticket. They helped drag me to the airplane the way in the movies you see those freaked-out prisoners being dragged to the gas chamber.

I was a mess. I was short-circuiting all over the place. Talking to myself, to Ramona, to Kathie, to God. "Help! Help. Help!" Great distress prevailed until the captain of AA Flight 628 came over to see what was going on.

My friend Larry stayed with me while Bill tried to convince the captain that I was in fact more than a minor celebrity who had a performance to do that night in New York City, to which he replied, "I don't care who he is. Do you know what it costs to land this plane in Kansas?"

At last—and I don't know how Bill pulled this off—he convinced the captain that I was behaving the way I was because I was rehearsing for a psychotic role. I was trying to get in character for a new Martin Scorsese movie. So the captain let me on!

When I got back to the loft, Ramona was in her nightgown and she seemed extremely sad but clear. She told me I had waited too long to come back. She had decided to move in with a girl friend until she could figure out what her next step should be. Then she told me she had decided to leave me, and when she said that, something broke. It was as if a dam had burst above my eyes, and I felt tears flowing like a river. I was wet with tears.

When Ramona walked out of what was now really my loft, she took all the feeling with her. The room turned into a dumb, dry desert and I sat there like a dead thing. Even when I cried I felt nothing but the wetness of tears, and I realized that all these years I had been letting Ramona feel for me. She did it so well. When there was the slightest emptiness of feeling in the room she filled it with her great heart, so there had been no space for my little, slow feelings to grow. I only had room for the panic feelings. It was as though I was squeezed between Ramona's feelings and my lack of them.

I had been invaded by an ocean of heart. And now I felt like a dead thing.

I grabbed a bottle of Stolichnaya peppered vodka, that fine red drink, and poured it straight into me. Then the room got very quiet and I could feel my breath, and I was suddenly calm and open to a new world of which I had been in deep denial. I wanted to see my son; after all, I'd never seen him and now he was eight months old. I was completely unaware that this was a long time. I was under the naïve impression that once a baby, always a baby. I guess I thought of six years old as the end of babyhood. I had no idea that eight months was quite a way along in the development of a child.

I called Kathie and went to see them. She woke the baby, lifted him out of the crib, and he went right for her breast. When I saw that, I knew there was no need for a blood test. I saw the back of my father's head in his head. I saw my brother Rocky's eyes. I saw a distant mirror, I saw a little lust flower. I saw a glorious accident. I saw a completely formed, whole human being, and I experienced a perfect paradox at that moment: I knew now that I could die and that I had to stay alive to help this little guy through.

Kathie had a radical plan. She said, "You haven't

seen him for eight months, you should go bond with him. Take him off alone, to your summer house in the country." And I did. I thought it was a completely mad idea, but I didn't question it. I was on the train to Brewster North with this eight-month-old creature, who was in my arms. I assumed he was beautiful, because everyone on the train kept stopping to say, "Oh my goodness, what a lovely granddaughter you have." And when I got up to the house, I put him on the floor like a rug rat, a hamster, a cat or a dog—let him do his thing; while I do my thing—get out the Bloody Mary mix, the salmon, the green peas and prepare dinner. And then I had to change his diaper. Bending over him, I looked down into his eyes, and fell in. I did not expect the gaze that came back, it was absolutely forever. Long, pure, empty, not innocent, because way beyond innocence, mere being, pure consciousness, the observing self that I'd always been trying to catch was staring back at me; they were no-agenda eyes. Clear, open, not blinking, not judging, not tempting, not needing, not hurting, not consoling. Just pure—not old, not new, because not in time. And I just stared until *I* blinked. And had to pull away. I couldn't go on anymore in there.

I took him in my arms and we were together for five hours. He ate with me, in my lap. And when I chewed my green peas, he reached into my mouth and took them out to feed himself. I got the image of Mother Bird,

Mother Robin, the way they spit the food into their babies' mouths. So I took his little head and, holding it, went to spit the green peas into his mouth like a mother bird, and he gave me a straight arm. And I thought, My God, he's got boundaries! Where would he get them at eight months? I could learn something from him. His dad doesn't have them at fifty-two! I would have just leaned back, opened my mouth, and cried, "Feed me!"

I put on a Bob Dylan CD and I took him out on the lawn and we spun round and round. He spun with centrifugal force, and then the centrifugal force reversed and he came in and I felt our hearts hitch up. And I thought, Oh yes, till death do us part. This innocent little Archimedes had a fulcrum big enough to split the fusion. A fusion I never dreamed I ever wanted split between Ramona and me. No woman could have done it; no other woman could've done it because back then there was often and always another woman, over my shoulder, over there, over there, but there's never just "another son." You don't say, "Hey, look at that son. Hey, look at the tush on that son!"

Everything was changing because of Forrest. I had thought that Ramona's leaving was the best thing she had ever done for herself and that now she would come into herself, finally. Her child would come into being and grow; she could find her work outside my shadow. I thought we would all be separate adults. My plan was that Kathie would live down the street, Ramona would be in her apartment, and I would be this independent bachelor with boundaries. But it didn't happen that way.

I was going out on a long tour, and I invited Kathie and the children to stay in my loft while I was gone. I never expect to come back from these tours. I'm always amazed—you know, metal fatigue, U.S. Air 737's. I'm always amazed when that plane lands on the tarmac and I'm back! And what a shock when I got to my little loft and it was bedlam. For years when I came back from tours, Ramona had a candlelight table setting, all my favorite imported beers on the table, broccoli rabe, a swanky gourmet dish. What I was seeing now was another world. Marissa, Kathie's daughter, is acting like a little indifferent opera-singing diva as I come into my loft . . . Why did I think everyone would be sitting like statues. Even an oversize cable TV could not calm this mob. Whoo-ee, what a scene.

Marissa was wearing her mother's dress, singing an epic improvised opera of her life. Kathie was running around, shouting ignored commands like a female ship captain to a crew of deaf sailors in a storm. Forrest jumped up on my desk and deposited a beautiful wet turd, and I almost ran. "How am I ever going to write?" I screamed. I thought he had gotten into the habit. I didn't know it was just a passing phase.

And there was a new kind of love going around in this new family. It was so different from the one-on-one, the only love I'd known before. This love alternated like a chain of broken-circuit Christmas lights. I loved Marissa for the way she loved her brother, my son. I loved my son Forrest for the way he loved Kathie, his mom, and turned her into a mother before I could, leaving me to get to know and love her for the woman she is.

I wanted to bring Forrest to my original home. I wanted to bring him to New England to see him in the landscape I'd grown up in. I wanted to bring him home to my—what? I was going to say "family." What family? My father had died just three days after I saw Forrest for the first time, died not knowing he had his first grandson. I didn't even know he was in the hospital dying, because my stepmother didn't call me due to the fact that she was so angry with me for the way I portrayed her in my novel, *Impossible Vacation*. I changed her name, but she recognized the details. She even tried to arrange my father's memorial service on a day I couldn't come, so I rearranged my tour to get there. When I got there, I felt the overwhelming importance of being there. Both my brothers read beautiful eulogies to my father. And I wanted to get up and say something—I'd written nothing—just say something impromptu. I got up and told about the last time I'd returned to New England and seen my father when he was still in decent health. He was seventy-nine then. He died at eighty-one.

I'd come back to do a theater workshop with New York City kids on Block Island. My father lived near the train station in Kingston, Rhode Island, and I asked him to pick me up and drive me to the Block Island ferry. I thought we could have a good visit in the car. At the train station Dad gave me that old obligatory bundle-of-wire hug and then we rode in silence, nothing to say except "No one's left." His best man had died the week before. Now he'd survived everyone. He and his wife had given up reading the obituaries. We rode in silence. Close to the ferry, he said, "You know, Rock—Chan—Spud"—whenever he forgot which son he was with, he called all three names out—"I was thinking, if we miss the ferry, we could have a beer together."

"What do you mean, Dad?"

"We could go to my summer cottage, if we miss the ferry."

"Well, let's miss it."

"What do you mean?"

"I can get another one in an hour!"

Every summer my stepmother and father would rent a cottage by the sea and never use it. They'd just leave it locked up; it was like an idea. And he wanted to go to it. So I said, "Let's go," and he did a U-turn in the car—I'd never seen him do that—and off we went. He opened the cottage for the first time that summer and it was all mildewed in there, and he got out the cocktail munchies. They were all fog-bound: wilted Cheez Doodles, soggy pretzels, those lite peanuts that are like Styrofoam, and two teeny cans of Budweiser—not my favorite beer, and not my favorite-size can. But it was a drink with Dad! We went to the picnic table out back near the water's edge and, oh God, this heavy Rhode Island fog was coming in: thick, pea-soup fog. It was like the opening of a Eugene O'Neill play.

We sat there in silence until I broke it and said, "Well, Dad, I guess it's good we have this chance to talk. I don't think we've talked since I was fourteen and you told me the facts of life on the golf course. But I was wondering, now that you're about to be eighty, do you have any regrets? Because I sometimes feel that my life is ruled by regret. I have so many. Do you have any, Dad?"

"Nope. Just that I never climbed Mt. Katahdin." (*sound of foghorn*)

"You know, Gram Gray once told me that you and Mom were married in the white church in Barrington on Halloween. What a kinky, imaginative day to get married on. Why'd you do that, Dad?"

"Seemed as good a day as any." (*sound of foghorn*)

"You know, you had three children, you had three boys. I never had any children, I don't know why—I don't know if it's by mistake or that I'm afraid to have them, or if I can't have them. What did you get out of having them, why would anyone have children?"

"That was the thing to do in those days." (*sound of foghorn*)

"Well, I won't bother you anymore. But I did want to ask you one more question. You had three boys, I was the middle son. Dad, why was I the only one that wasn't circumcised?" (*long pause*)

"You weren't?"

Then I said, "Well, I guess we better get going."

And Dad said, "Oh, all right, pack it up. Yep, yep. Lock up, lock up."

We got outside and he realized he hadn't called my stepmother, Sis, to find out what kind of fish to bring home from the Galilee market, and he said, "Oh shit! I forgot to call Sis." Then he unlocked the door and went back in to call, and I thought, My father never said "shit" in front of me in his life. He came back out and I realized I'd left my Danish school bag in there. The cottage was locked up again and I said, "Oh shit, Dad, I left my Danish school bag in there." And then I realized we had just bonded. Those two "shits" made all the difference. I told this story at my father's memorial service. I did. My stepmother said afterward, "You're crazy. You're on drugs. Your father never said that word in his life. Don't you ever come back to Rhode Island as long as you live!"

I had visions of my stepmother guarding the Rhode Island border with a pith helmet on and a huge barbecue fork in each hand, I couldn't bring my son back to that, so I said, The hell with it. Then I thought, Why this big hang-up about Rhode Island? Try to think about New England in a larger perspective. Kathie had family in New England. Her sister Karen was a ski instructor at Stowe. We could return to New England by the northern route, and go back to Vermont, not Rhode Island. Go back on skis. A family that skis together might just stay together. Kathie was a good skier; her daughter, Marissa, was learning, and Forrest had potential. Kathie had given me skis for Christmas and I would go early. I would go a day early and finally live out the fantasy of finding my balance on skis in New England. It's just a short flight up from Newark on Continental Air to Burlington. Didn't have to fly all the way to Tahoe. At last I could ski with my people.

I was sitting in Newark Airport having a beer and waiting for the flight to Burlington, when I heard: "Continental Flight 451 will be delayed for about five minutes." I have another beer and I hear: "Continental

Flight 451 will be delayed for another five minutes," and I pipe up and say, "Excuse me, when you say five minutes, what do you mean—twenty, forty, what?"

The ticket agent says, "Quiet down, please."

And I say, "No, I'm really curious. You also keep saying, 'Delayed, delayed, delayed.' We'd really like to know why it's delayed."

Then I turn to the rest of the people waiting for Flight 451 and say, "Wouldn't we be more forgiving if we could all hear the story from you rather than see it on CNN or something? What are you, sheep?"

And the agent yells, "Quiet!"

Then there's a pause and we hear: "Continental Flight 451 will be delayed due to heavy rains in Orlando."

"All right!" I yell. "Do you see what a difference that makes? Now we have an image of the plane on glistening black tarmac and of the rain coming down, the pilot sitting there . . ."

And the ticket agent cuts me with another big "Quiet!"

Continental Flight 451 was delayed, very delayed. They bumped me to first class, probably because they were afraid I'd start a revolution in coach. There was no one in there with me, and we were late and I was all fuzzy, cranky, and out of it, and there we were, at last, in the Burlington Airport, and I was trying to focus and concentrate on all I had to do to get out and on to Stowe. And oh, there go my skis on the baggage carousel.

I get on the phone. "Is Hertz still open? I got my rent-a-car number here somewhere. Oh no, it's Avis." Oh damn it all. Oh, I need a woman. I need an organized woman to organize my life. I can't—uh—wait! I see the baggage carousel stop and I hear: "The baggage carousel has now officially stopped for the night. Please collect your skis at the baggage claim."

"No!" I flip out and scream, "Please, the skis are just on the other side of the rubber curtain!" They ignore me and make the same announcement again. And I yell out to the empty airport, "I know you can see me! Turn that carousel on!"

I go over to complain at the Continental baggage claim desk and say, "Continental Air? Do you know, I sometimes write for *Traveler* magazine, and the next article I write, the first thing I'll talk about is how bad you guys operate!"

"Oh, do you really," responds the agent behind the desk. "Well, my husband just had dinner with the governor of Vermont. What does that make me? I've had a hard day, too."

And just like that, we are going at it.

And this little old lady behind me, who has to be the original Vermont Maid on the syrup bottle, says, "I wonder why people who don't like Vermont come here?"

At this point the woman behind the baggage desk pushes a button and I see two armed guards with two German shepherds coming for me, and I gasp and cry out, "Oh my God, I thought I was in Vermont, not New Hampshire!" I am so thrown by this that by the time I finally get the rent-a-car and am on my way, I drive straight past Exit 10 to Stowe and end up in Montpelier.

Five hours later, the time it takes to fly to Tahoe, I drive into Stowe at one in the morning. I can't wake up Karen, Kathie's sister. I've got to check into a hotel. What do I find? The Buttermilk Inn. It's like a Republican rest home. It's like it was built in 1776 yesterday. Vinyl clapboard siding, little narrow beds, steam heat coming up that I can't turn off. So I open the windows wide enough to let in cold air. In the morning all I can see is the ghost of Mom rushing in to snap up the window shade and cry, "This is the day the Lord hath made, let us rejoice and be happy in it!" And I'm trying to be happy in it. Grumble, grumble, grumble. Outside are big snowbanks, made up from eighteen snowstorms, now all black and crusted and dirty.

I go to the dining room for breakfast. The waitresses are all dressed like colonial theme park Betsy Ross/*Gone with the Wind* dolls. They've got so many ruffles on them I can't tell the bed from the breakfast. The other skiers are all staggering around the "all you can eat" breakfast smorgasbord like somnambulistic J. Crew models. The breakfast looks like a picture from the menu: canary-yellow, dry scrambled eggs; turkey bacon done in a microwave; dry toast; generic coffee so weak you can see to the bottom of the cup—it takes me eight cups to get out of my chair!

I get my ski outfit and think, What am I doing here? This place is too weird. Remember you've come back to New England to ski. I step outside into bone-chilling, damp air and flat light, gray flat light. Mt. Mansfield looks like a low dome, not the sunstruck peaks of the West. And as I drive to the slope I see tangled trees, nothing like the aspens with the light coming through them. Tangled, weird, dark trees. Oh, *Crucible* trees, "Mary Warren dancing naked around a cauldron, dropping a frog into the pot" trees.

I drive to the lodge and buy my ticket—what a scene! They've had eighteen snowstorms, and the ski-lift operators are depressed. They look like Department of Public Works employees; there's no rock'n'roll music. Their shoulders are hunched. They're dressed in black. They've got yellow caution bars on their back. I buy a ticket, which they don't even check because they don't care.

I start up the lift and the first thing that occurs to me is fear of slow-lift thoughts. Unlike the West, this place has a history for me. Don't let it come back to me now. Oh Jesus, Johnnie-Walker-home-for-the-holidays picture. Oh, look out there: Ethan Allen/Ethan Frome hills. Oh, but look down: no condos around. Just a ski lodge that's really simple. Looks like a log cabin. And oh, there, hey look: a working farm. A red barn tucked away in a snowdrift. This place has a history, it was a place before it was a resort. Now, farther up on the lift, I see the village of Stowe, like a Norman Rockwell Monopoly town. And there, the white steeple of a church like the one Mom and Dad were married in on Halloween. I remember photographs of their honeymoon, the moose hunt in Maine. And the memories of their skis —they had wooden skis then. They must've skied up here. But they never took us skiing, or told us about it.

And now the memory of Dad in summer in his vegetable garden, and I can see him picking green peas across from Mom, who's raking her flower garden, both of them in harmony then. Five of us living in harmony, and the seasons going around like a wheel, not a line, but a circle, giving us our moods, giving us our personalities. Autumn, sad, sweet, sharp air, spinning into winter—cozy, muffle of white—into spring—moist, sprouting, hope—into summer—timeless, long, sea days, jingle of crickets—into night, into autumn: a wheel. Not a line. And no place else in mind, no West, no could-be-there or could-be-here, just HERE, the five of us in harmony. And at Christmas, the whole family, seventeen of us around the big table.

And then the memory of that last Christmas: Mom not there; Mom, who took my hand, pointed to beauty, and led me to beauty, had taken herself out of the world and was no longer the centerpiece of our Christmas, and no one talking about it, no one acknowledging her mammoth absence, except my brother Rocky, who has been drinking too much and can't deal with it and is saying, "What about Mom?" And my Grandmother Horton responding, "She's in heaven now, dear. She's better off there." And my grandfather saying, "Don't speak about her. Don't speak about that, not a word." And Rocky getting so drunk I had to take him outside to air his head. And now out behind my grandparents' house I discover a construction site. And a dump truck. I see the key in the ignition. I help Rocky in. I show him how to start it and I aim him like a terrorist bomber at my grandparents' house. Roaring off, he grazes the white picket fence! Scrapes the willow tree, and comes to a crashing rest in the azaleas by their house! While all the time my grandfather and grandmother are doing their heart-attack dance in the window.

"Oh shit!" I forgot to raise the safety bar on the lift! I forgot in the East they have these safety bars. I almost didn't get off, and oh God, it's sugar and ice, mashed potatoes. Oh my God, boom, boom, boom; oh, crud ruts, no fun without the sun. Can't see with my bad eye in this flat light. Oh, plop, I'm down, and my ass is wet. And I'm up again, and all of a sudden I'm down the mountain. What was that? What the hell was that? Sixteen minutes up and three minutes down.

I don't know, I'll ride up again—nothing else to do. Think I'll ride with a guy this time, be social (*long silence*). All right. If he's not going to talk to me, I won't talk to him. I don't have to talk. We can ride in silence. I'm not afraid of silence. I hear the sound of the cable over the pulley. And the silence turns to sadness. Not a depression, but a deep sadness, and I think, Let it go, you can let it go. Don't long for that day, the memory of the perfect skiing day with Barney in that California light. You are not there now, you're here. Let that one go. Let go of the memory of Ramona, the remorse you feel for what you did to her, and how her bright lights will never never shine on you again. Let that one go. Let go of the memory of Mom's madness. Let go of the memory of Dad dying alone, without me and his grandson Forrest beside him.

And another layer of sadness peels off and drifts down behind me like a great gray gossamer web upon the snow below. And I think, No one really knows anything. No one's watching us. No one's watching over us. And I will die. And you will die. And one by one all the stars will go out in the sky.

And oh, ah—I'm up and off! Oh, the wonderful impingencies of the snow! What a great mountain! It has
a personality. Look at that, a big patch of blood over
there. It looks like the poor mountain is bleeding. And
around it I ski. You know what I like about this mountain? I'm thinking, It's really without bowls, it's filled
with trails that reveal the mountain as I go. It's a discreet
and cozy revelation. You never know what's coming
next. It's like white-water rafting, only the river is frozen. And look, I'm on Upper Lord now and going down
Center Line. Hey, this is a steep one. Ooh, someone just
fell next to me. Wasn't me. I didn't fall, I don't have to
fall. I'm making it, I'm on Lower Lord now. And I'm
skiing along the edge of the trees. Isn't that interesting?
How the trees now give dimension to the snow? And
I'm thinking this and skiing at the same time. It's not
as flat if I'm skiing by the trees. No, not the same flat
light, and down into Lower Lord, I'm just doing wide,
playful, meaningless sweeps from one side to the other,
and oops, I slip back on my skis: a perfect ACL ripping
move, but I'm up again! And my knees are all right, and
oh, I'm down the mountain!

Not bad, I'm beginning to like it. Beginning to understand this mountain. Every mountain has its own personality. Time for lunch. I go to meet Kathie's sister,
Karen. I have a well-done hamburger, and Karen tells

me she's too busy setting up the downhill race course to work with me but we should meet later at Spruce Peak just across the road and take a run together.

I finish lunch and go into the men's room to take a whiz. I'm looking at the guy next to me. I rarely do this, but he's got a strange poncho on, or what? What the hell is he wearing? It looks kind of trashy. He's got beads of water on it. He turns to me and says, "Garbage-bag weather. Don't want to be a fair-weather skier, do ya?"

"Nope!"

I walk outside and it's raining and everyone is coming down the mountain in garbage bags! They're flapping like plastic bags in the wind! I think, Oh my God, imagine this in Aspen! I like this place, and I'm skiing in the rain in a garbage bag. I've never done anything in my life in the rain, and now I'm doing it in a garbage bag, and I'm paying to do it!

At the end of a wild-weather day—I've experienced all the elements but sun, and of course now the rain has turned to ice—I meet Karen and we ski Spruce Peak. No one's out there but the two of us, and she's a magnificent skier; she's doing just beautiful carved turns on ice. It sounds as if we're both defrosting a giant refrigerator. After we finish, I invite Karen to come with me to celebrate at the Fox and Hound, an English pub in

Stowe that looks like a tornado hit it in England and brought it, with all its merry revelers, and plopped it down in Stowe. There's a Scottish ski instructor from Glasgow who's come in early to watch *Star Trek*. His name is Scotty and he's a Trekkie! He's got a kilt on; he says he has no underwear underneath it. He says, "Oh, isn't it a wild thing when that white stuff flies up and tickles your bum." And over in the corner there's an old man playing chess with a young boy. There's a man, smoking a pipe, reading Ralph Waldo Emerson essays. There are two ladies having tea. There's a bartender speaking in complete sentences. What is right with this picture? It's my new eccentric clubhouse. I'm glad to be back in odd old New England.

The following day Kathie arrives with the children: Forrest, who is now eighteen months, and Marissa, her daughter, who is seven. Marissa and I are not getting along very well at this point, because among other things, the problem is that we're both self-absorbed drama queens. There is no time we are not acting. I see it in her, she picks it up in me. And not only are we competing for the same woman, her mom, but we are also learning how to ski at the same time and we are both strange attractors. All we have to do is stand next to each other and we crash into one another. We could be standing still and we'd crash; it was as if we had negative-negative supermagnets in our ski boots. She'd ski over the back of my skis and crash and cry, "Mommy, Mommy, he did it again! How am I ever going to make a living?"

So off Marissa goes with Karen, to learn how to ski. Forrest is in daycare, so Kathie and I at last get a rare break to ski together. I'm in a foul mood. I'm just in one of those "Oh God, nothing is perfect because New England isn't the West" modes. "And, yeah, if you can learn to ski in New England, you can ski anywhere, and you won't be able to wait to get anywhere." I'm saying the sun hasn't come out since I've been here and I'm suffering from SAD, Seasonal Affective Disorder. I looked it up in the *Mayo Clinic Family Health Book*.

And Kathie is saying, "Spalding, you're really spoiled. You have a good life. Be thankful. Be thankful it's not raining." It begins to rain. She says, "Be thankful it's not cold." It begins to get cold. "Be thankful the wind isn't blowing." The wind begins to blow. So we have the new New England prayer: Be thankful for what hasn't happened yet.

And up we go. It's raining down below, but the weatherman is predicting snow at a thousand feet. And damn it all if that isn't what's happening. It's like a seventh-grade science project. There is almost an exact line where you can see the rain turn to snow. I'm trying to catch it. And because it's raining down below, not many people are skiing that day. Kathie and I are up at the top alone. We are in my favorite condition, I realize, new snow falling. Not a heavy storm with wind, so that it's driving in your face, but a steady light snow that just covers our tracks so that each time up we are making fresh ones. And for the first time, we no longer have the sound of our skis cutting ice. We have only that silent sound of snow falling and a kind of cozy creak—the skis on new snow. Like when my Grandfather Horton would motor out in his sailboat in Narragansett Bay, then turn the motor off and hoist the sail, and there would only be wind.

Kathie was skiing ahead of me, very contemplative, easygoing, making tracks; there before me, dressed in wet faded dungarees and a garbage bag. She'd stop at different places and look out for no reason at all but to gaze over the landscape. And I'd pull in beside her and stop and look out, too, feeling no sadness now in the sound of the wind. The birches beside us took on a purple hue from a milky sun trying to break through.

After skiing together, we went to meet Karen and Marissa over at Spruce Peak, for the final run of the day. Skiing down Spruce Peak, we fall into this new constellation, like an inverted triangle; it's as if the old Fryeburg geometry-class triangle is coming home to this mountain. Karen and Kathie make up the base of the inverted triangle. Marissa is in the center, but she's also triangulated because she is doing the perfect snowplow. And I am at the apex. We somehow manage to stay in this configuration all the way, and halfway down the mountain I find I am so balanced that I am also able to turn and look over my shoulder to see Marissa. Her eyes are totally focused, and she's got her poles lifted high. And Marissa looks so great. She is snowplowing straight down that mountain with her ski poles held just right in front of her and she has this great gleeful look on her face. I can't stand it. I cry out and from my mouth come words I have never heard in my life: "Go for it, Marissa! You're doing great! You're really skiing great!"

Where did that totally supportive, non-ironic voice come from? Where did that wholesome cheerleader voice come from? Not from me! Nor could I ever remember those words being spoken to me. What a foreign voice, and there it was, along with a burst of sun that shone like an amber floodlight etched against a gray sky to illuminate our last run.

Everyone wanted to quit and pick up Forrest. I needed one last run alone, because now I had good slow-lift thoughts. A good feeling. I thought, That's incredible, that non-ironic voice born here in Vermont. That's it! Maybe I could at last retire from endless touring of confessional monologues and become a ski instructor for children. Move to Vermont with my family. At last be in one place and have a private life. Have some connection before I die.

And now, skiing down the mountain and ready to test that new voice again, I see a little boy ahead of me, snowplowing. Behind him, without his knowledge, I scream out, "Go for it, guy, you're doing great!" And he turns and CRASH! He's down! Kiddie yard sale! I help him up and apologize.

When I rejoin the family at the bottom of the slope, everyone is concerned because they have heard that a big dump is on it's way—the nineteenth snowstorm of the season. I drive Kathie to the airport to try to beat the storm. Marissa has to go to school and Kathie has to get back to work. And ski bum that I fantasize I am, I am staying on for the big one.

And it is a big one! People are saying they're ready to commit suicide if it hits. It's a Monday and it's April Fools' Day and no one's on the mountain. I am so excited. It's fifteen degrees below with the windchill. Out of the gondola, the wind sweeps me like an ice boat across boilerplate ice onto Upper Perry Merrill and then into heavy powder, and I'm down. And I'm up again. I've never skied in snow like this before. My skis get caught in it and turn up the slope so that I end up going down the slope backwards. It's like a slapstick silent movie in white. Now I'm skiing well again until I hit a snowdrift. My skis go right into it and I'm projected like a shot from a cannon into a white world and, plop, I'm in deep and I'm all hot and sweaty and up comes a memory from childhood—hot in our snowsuits, buried under piles of snow, feeling oh so warm and sleepy in all that cold and cozy white. Why not let it all go and cuddle on down deep, deep into snow, the sound of the bare wind above it all. Wind tearing at frozen birches. Not a bad way to go. To fall asleep in fresh snow forever.

"No, no, find your skis," some commanding adult voice in me persists. "Find your skis and return to your family."

I stagger out of my snow grave to dig for my skis, jabbing my poles deep into the snow to try to make contact, until at last, sweating and exhausted, I pull them both out and carefully step into the bindings and step firmly down to begin again. Down the endless white run.

All day, I hardly see a skier on the slope. The light barely changes and I have no idea what time it is. It's white time turning into white-out. I can no longer tell the difference between the sky and the slope, except for my red skis, which serve as an occasional boundary.

Now, spent and exhausted by this absolute emptied-out day, I'm skiing down and see ahead a yellow figure that I immediately intuit to be a man. From a distance, he looks like a displaced fisherman. He's in a yellow macintosh, oilcloth slicker, and yellow oilcloth pants, and he is doing the most beautiful, carved, Tai Chi–like turns, just meditative skiing. I fall behind him doing the same. Unaware, he's become my new teacher. Because he doesn't see me, he doesn't know he's teaching me, and because of this I'm able to really work with him. Halfway down the mountain I ski in beside him and see that this man is in his seventies. In great shape, he has dancing eyes, and I say to him, "Thank you for the lesson."

And he says, "Oh, my pleasure. I didn't know you were behind me. How are you doing?"

And I say, "To tell the truth, I don't know if I'm having a good time or trying to kill myself."

He says, "When you're in that place that's when you know you're alive."

And I bid him farewell and ski down, knowing I have seen both a person and an apparition, the spirit of the future. That I, too, could be skiing at seventy, if I continued, if I took care of myself, skiing with my son if he wanted to ski.

Coming in at the end of the day, I thought, I've come back to an old place in a new way. I thought I was going to self-destruct and instead I helped bring new life into the world. I gave myself a big high five, and I thought, You know, I've returned to New England and I'm no longer a puritan, if you define a puritan as someone who is constantly haunted by the sneaky suspicion that someone, somewhere else, is having a good time.

A NOTE ABOUT THE AUTHOR

Writer, actor, and performer, SPALDING GRAY is the author of *Swimming to Cambodia*, *Gray's Anatomy*, *Monster in a Box*, and *Sex and Death to the Age 14*, among other works. He has appeared on PBS and HBO, and in numerous films, including Roland Joffe's *The Killing Fields*, David Byrne's *True Stories*, and, most recently, Steven Soderbergh's *Gray's Anatomy*.

It's a Slippery Slope premiered in November 1996 at the Vivian Beaumont Theater in New York City and was performed around the United States and the United Kingdom.